ENGLAND'S  HEROES

First published in the UK in 2026 by Dino Books,
an imprint of Bonnier Books UK,
5th Floor, HYLO, 105 Bunhill Row,
London, EC1Y 8LZ
www.bonnierbooks.co.uk

X @UFHbooks
www.heroesfootball.com

Text copyright © Studio Press 2026

1 3 5 7 9 10 8 6 4 2

Paperback ISBN: 978-1-78946-937-0
E-book ISBN: 978-1-78946-972-1

The authorised representative in the EEA is Bonnier Books UK (Ireland) Limited.
Registered office address: Block B, The Crescent Building
Northwood, Santry
Dublin 9, D09 C6X8, Ireland
compliance@bonnierbooks.ie

A CIP catalogue record for this book is available from the British Library

Typeset by Envy Design Ltd.

Printed and bound in Great Britain by CPI (UK) Ltd, Croydon CR0 4YY

TOM PALMER

ULTIMATE FOOTBALL HEROES

ENGLAND'S HEROES

FROM THE PLAYGROUND TO THE PITCH

Tom Palmer is the author of 58 books for children, including six prize-winning WWI and WWII novels and four football series, *Roy of the Rovers*, *Football Academy*, *Foul Play* and *The Soccer Diaries*. He works in schools up and down the UK promoting reading for pleasure through football. www.tompalmer.co.uk

Cover illustration by Dan Leydon.
To learn more about Dan, visit danleydon.com
To purchase his artwork visit etsy.com/shop/footynews
Or just follow him on X @danleydon

For Lennon Robinson, to mark your
first World Cup

This book is about the England men's senior football team. Written in time for you to read it before the 2026 World Cup.

I hope you enjoy it. And I really hope you enjoy the World Cup.

The first World Cups I remember – as a child – were Germany 1974 and Argentina 1978. The main thing I remember, though, is that England weren't there. And that was disappointing.

So when we did get there (Spain 1982) it was amazing. But I was 14. Just one World Cup tournament in my childhood.

So… enjoy it. Please. Even if it goes horribly wrong for England, you can still support those countries featuring players from the club you support.

I have been lucky enough to meet five of the footballers mentioned in this book.

I had an argument with the first about whether

reading is worth the effort. He was wrong.

I almost… so nearly… spilled a drink on the second.

The third and I had a heated argument. At school. We were 15.

The fourth didn't take my advice and might have regretted it.

The fifth accidentally took my referee's whistle.

These events happened over a 30-year period. It was an honour to meet them all!

Thanks to my friends and football experts, Simon Robinson, Jim Sells and David Luxton.

And thanks to you too, for reading this book.

Tom

THE FIRST INTERNATIONAL FOOTBALL MATCH... EVER

1872

England's first official football match took place on 30 November 1872. It was played in Scotland. And it was Scotland's first football match too.

That is because Scotland v England 1872 was the first international football game ever played.

The game was played at Hamilton Crescent in Glasgow. On a cricket pitch.

But, although it is recognised by FIFA as the first full international between the two countries, England and Scotland had already played five representative matches against each other in the previous two years. All of those took place in London and – because it was a time before cars and buses and motorways – the teams in those first games included only Scottish players who were based in southern England.

For the record, England won two and drew three of those five games. They had lost none.

Could England remain undefeated in Glasgow? In front of 4,000 passionate Scots? Especially as all the Scottish players played for the same team, Queen's Park, then the top club in Scotland?

Yes, they could.

Although the Scots had the best of the first half, the English bossed the second half and the game ended 0–0.

The England team was made up of men from universities and the army, as well as footballers from Notts County, Sheffield Wednesday and Crystal Palace.

There are no videos or photographs of the game, but there are some pretty funny drawings of the players battling for the ball. Remember – this was a long time ago. Queen Victoria was in the 35th year of her near 64-year reign over the British Empire. And, in those times, cameras were bigger than footballers and they didn't work outside.

1873

England's first goal was scored by a man who was born in India. His name was William Kenyon-Slaney.

He scored it during the second-ever international football game on 8 March 1873. The game was, like the first international, played between England and Scotland. This time it took place in London, at the Oval. Another cricket ground.

William Kenyon-Slaney had had an interesting life.

He was born in Rajkot in 1847, when India was firmly part of the British Empire. He was a decorated soldier, having been in the British Army. He was educated at Eton College and Oxford University. And in later life he was a Member of Parliament for 22 years.

He also played first-class cricket.

Not only did Kenyon-Slaney score England's first

goal on that day in 1873 – he scored a second time as England beat Scotland 4–2 that day.

He was never selected to play for England again, which means his goal average stands at two goals per game.

ENGLAND'S BIGGEST WIN

1882

England fans only had to wait ten years after their first
international game for their biggest win.

13–0!

The team travelled across the Irish sea by ship to
play Ireland in Belfast.

This was 37 years before passenger flights were
introduced and 69 years before England travelled to
their first football game by air.

It would also be another 39 years before 1921,
when Ireland would be divided into two: Northern
Ireland and what we now know as the Republic of
Ireland. So, in this game, England played the whole
of Ireland.

This was, in fact, Ireland's first game as a country.
Their team was made up largely of footballers from
two teams, Knock FC and Cliftonville. But it was early

days for Ireland who had only established a football association two years earlier, in 1880. Whereas England had formed theirs in 1863.

Prior to this date England had played 13 games, all against Scotland or Wales. They had won 4 of them, drawn 2 and lost 7, including a 6–1 home defeat to Scotland in their previous game.

Even so, England outclassed the Irish here, leading to their largest victory. The game included the first two hat-tricks in international football. The first by Arthur Brown (who scored 4 goals), and the second by Howard Vaughton (who scored 5).

Both Brown and Vaughton played for Aston Villa.

Yet England's euphoria in the light of their win would be short lived. The following month, England were slaughtered 5–1 by Scotland and well beaten 5–3 by Wales.

FOOTBALL AGAINST FOREIGNERS!

1908

England's first 94 games had been played exclusively in the British Isles, against Scotland, Wales and Ireland. They had won 58, drawn 18 and lost 18 of those games.

But the English Football Association wanted to test their players against continental opposition. Could they do as well in Europe? That was one reason for their first-ever European tour.

But there were other reasons, too.

One was to spread the rules of English association football in a world that still had several different sets of footballing rules.

Another reason was to make friends with other countries, perhaps to avoid wars in future decades.

From 6–13 June 1908, England travelled to three amazing European capital cities. This was at a time when only the wealthy travelled abroad. Most people in England had never left their county, let alone their country.

Based on the scorelines, you could say the tour was a success for the England team. They beat Austria 6–1 and 11–1 in Vienna, Hungary 7–0 in Budapest, and Bohemia (now part of the Czech Republic) 4–0 in Prague.

But it was less of a success if it was intended to try and prevent wars.

Six years later, in what would be called the First World War, Britain would be involved in a very different kind of conflict with all three countries that England had beaten. Several of England's players would play significant roles – such as Jack Cock, who would survive the conflict, and Evelyn Lintott, who would not.

THE FIRST ENGLAND PLAYER TO FALL

1916

Evelyn Lintott was a Leeds City player, who had represented the England football team seven times. With six wins and one draw, he remained undefeated on the football field at international level.

A schoolteacher also, Lintott was one of the first footballers to sign up to fight in the First World War in 1914, and was quickly promoted to the rank of an officer, which meant he was a leader of men on the battlefield. He was a member of the West Yorkshire Regiment, also known as the Leeds Pals.

He fell on the first day of the Battle of the Somme. It was 1 July 1916 and he was one of over 19,000 British soldiers who lost their lives on that day alone.

The Yorkshire Post newspaper reported from a fellow soldier that he led his men bravely until his final breath.

There is a photograph of Evelyn Lintott wearing his England kit, possibly in his front garden. He has his foot on a ball and is smiling like a little boy who has been given his first football top.

Lest we forget.

JACK COCK

1919

The First World War lasted from 1914 to 1918. During the war no official England football matches were played.

Their international games only resumed in late 1919, almost a full year after the signing of the Armistice on 11 November 1918.

Their first game was against Ireland, away.

Seven of England's team were making their debut for their country. Five years is a long time in football. Some men from the team as it was before the war were too old to play for their country now. Some had been injured in the war, like former captain and centre forward, Jack Woodward. Some – like Edwin Latheron, James Conlin and Evelyn Lintott – never came home at all.

The England game against Ireland took place on

25 October 1919 at Windsor Park in Belfast.

One player making his debut was 25-year-old Jack Cock from Cornwall, a centre forward who had just signed for Chelsea from Huddersfield Town.

Cock had also fought at the Somme and many other battles for the so-called Footballers' Battalion.

Thirty seconds into his debut for his country he scored.

It is hard to imagine how he felt. Scoring for his country after having seen years of war in the trenches. But that is what Jack Cock did, and England had begun a new chapter in their footballing story.

WEMBLEY

1924

The first England game played at Wembley Stadium was a British International Championship tie with Scotland in April 1924.

The stadium was part of a huge complex of exhibitions, restaurants, museums and fairground rides built as part of the British Empire Exhibition in 1923.

The idea behind the exhibition was to celebrate the relationships between all the countries of the British Empire in a world still making sense of itself after the First World War. Already the British Empire was beginning to crumble. The war had changed everything.

The Wembley stadium with its twin towers was meant to be knocked down after the exhibition, but now, as the home of English football, it was agreed it would remain intact.

Unlike the British Empire.

England and Huddersfield Town keeper, Edward Taylor, will go down in history as the man who scored the first international goal at the iconic stadium. Unfortunately, it was an own goal – in favour of Scotland in a game that ended in a 1–1 draw.

JACK LESLIE

1925

In 2022 the family of Plymouth Argyle footballer Jack Leslie was awarded an honorary cap. This was 97 years after the player had been selected for England.

Why did it take so long?

Up until 1963 the England football team was chosen by a selection committee at the Football Association (FA), not the manager. In a time before the internet or even television, the selection committee had often not even seen their choices in action on the pitch.

And this is how the greatest injustice of England football selection took place.

Born in London, Jack Leslie played for Plymouth Argyle. He scored 134 goals in 284 appearances for the club, 74 of them alongside Jack Cock. After such exploits, Leslie's abilities were recognised by the FA in

London and he was selected to play for England in the 1925 British Home Championships.

But then, before a ball was kicked, he was dropped from the team.

It became clear that Jack was dropped because he was Black.

He said in later life, while working in the backroom staff at West Ham United, that they must have forgotten the colour of his skin.

Jack died in 1988. As well as his posthumous cap, he has a statue at Home Park in Plymouth, a road named after him, and a blue plaque marking where he was born in London. In 2022, he was inducted into the England football Hall of Fame in 2022.

But Jack Leslie never played for his country.

And after Jack was dropped from the England side, it would be another 53 years, 1978, before England's first Black player, Viv Anderson, would take to the field.

REVENGE

1931

If you include the 1908 tour of Austria, Hungary and Bohemia, England's first 24 games against teams outside the British Isles resulted in 23 wins and one draw.

They had to lose one day.

But it still took until 1929, 57 years after the first England international game for them to lose to a foreign team: a 4–3 defeat to Spain. Annoying, because England had been 3–2 up with just ten minutes to go.

Revenge was required.

The rematch against Spain took place two years later at Arsenal's Highbury Stadium.

And England's revenge was particularly sweet. They won 7–1.

One player who scored for England that day was

Dixie Dean, a prolific scorer at Everton with 349 goals in 399 games. He went on to score 18 goals in 16 appearances for England.

The year before England's triumph against Spain, the first World Cup had been played in Uruguay. But England did not enter the tournament that year. In fact, they did not enter the World Cup until 1950.

IN YOUR FACE, MUSSOLINI!

1933

It was the early 1930s. Europe was approaching its darkest times. Hitler would take power in Germany in 1933. And a second world war would come in 1939.

Fascist leader Benito Mussolini had been in charge of Italy since 1922, and by 1933 the former democracy was now a dictatorship.

In that year, England travelled to Rome to play Italy for the first time. They faced a team that would go on to win the second and third World Cups in 1934 and 1938.

An Italian footballer opened the scoring. His name was Giovanni Ferrari, and like the car of the same name, Ferrari acted quickly. His goal came after just four minutes.

But England's Cliff Bastin equalised on 23 minutes. A crisp shot, after coming in from the left wing.

It was a close game, though Italy forced the England keeper to make a string of fine saves. The game ended 1–1.

It was a great result – a score draw against the team that would win the next two World Cups. But the game is also remembered for the reaction of the Italian dictator, after a stray ball from England's Edris Hapgood hit him full in the face.

Mussolini was not amused.

Nor would he be pleased about what happened the next time the two teams met.

THE BATTLE OF HIGHBURY

1934

When the Italians came to England in 1934, they had just been crowned World Champions for the first time at the World Cup.

But, because England and the other home nations had not competed in the World Cup – and also because England were considered the best team in the world – the England v Italy match was seen as a chance to see who really was the best.

In the end the match would be remembered not for the result, but for how brutal it was. The England legend, Stanley Matthews, then in his early days as an international player, would call it the most violent match he had played in.

After two minutes of the game, the Italian centre half Luis Monti had his foot broken in a tackle by Ted Drake. Astonishingly, he played on for another 15 minutes. But, by the time he came off, England were 3–0 up – two goals from Eric Brook (Manchester City) after 3 and 10 minutes, and one from Drake (after 12 minutes) left the World Champions floundering.

The Italians were not happy how they had lost one of their team, and the match became very violent. England players left the stadium beaten up, with injuries to legs, arms, noses and hands. But did they hold onto their lead?

It was close. In the second half Italy launched a comeback. To give them credit, they had been down to ten men since Monti went off. (This was a time before substitutes had been invented.)

But it was not enough. The Battle of Highbury ended 3–2 to England. Proving – to some – that England were the best in the world.

Italy would go on to win the Olympic gold in 1936, and the next World Cup in 1938. But in June 1940, Italian dictator, Benito Mussolini (the one who got the ball in the face in 1933) declared hostilities against Britain, and the two countries were no longer in conflict on a football field, but on a battlefield.

BEATING SCOTLAND

1939

England had not won in Scotland for 12 years – and it was 1939.

Could England register a win before the inevitable war came and changed everything?

It seemed unlikely. In driving Scottish rain, England struggled to play with their natural flair. And on a heavily waterlogged pitch, they passed the ball back to their keeper, who was out of position, allowing Scotland to score an easy opener.

A terrible start for England. It was beginning to look like they would go longer than 12 years without a win in Scotland. This, in front of 149,269 fans, mostly a home crowd.

At half-time, and 1–0 down, England players were so drenched that they had to borrow a set of Queen's Park white away shirts for the second half.

Would wearing these shirts make a difference?
Could they bring England luck?

Maybe.

Because on 66 minutes, Pat Beasley of Huddersfield Town exploited a Scottish error and equalised for England. And then, with only a minute to go, Stanley Matthews crossed for Tommy Lawton to head the ball home.

A 2–1 win for England, it would be England and Scotland's last competitive game for seven years.

STAN MORTENSEN

1940

Stan Mortensen had a remarkable career for England. A prolific goal scorer, he netted 14 goals in his first eight games. Four of them on his debut.

Mortensen's place in the history of the England team is amplified by the fact that he played in arguably their two most infamous games. A 1–0 defeat to the USA in the 1950 World Cup finals. And the day at Wembley in 1953 when England were outplayed and outclassed by Hungary, who became the first foreign team to beat England at home.

We'll learn more about those games soon. But all this footballing history came after Stan Mortensen was told that he would never play football again.

It is another astonishing war story.

When still a teenager Mortensen was a wireless operator on board a Second World War Wellington

Bomber when it crashed. The pilot and the bomb aimer were killed. The navigator lost a leg. And Mortensen was told his head injuries meant that his footballing days were over.

Yet just three weeks later, he was playing for the RAF Football team.

In surviving such a horrific accident, Stan Mortensen went on to score 23 goals in 25 appearances for England. He will go down in history as the first England player to score in a World Cup qualifier (against Wales in 1949) and the first to score in the World Cup finals (against Chile the following year).

This from the man who was told he would never play again.

There is a statue of Mortensen outside Blackpool FC's Bloomfield Road Stadium. He scored 197 goals for Blackpool between 1941 and 1955.

SIR TOM FINNEY, TANK BATTLE SURVIVOR

1942

Many England footballers gave up professional football between the years 1939 and 1945. They did this to fight in the Second World War.

Tom Finney was one such player. He was only 17 at the beginning of the war and was playing for Preston North End. He did this while also working as a plumber.

But in 1942, aged 20, he was called up to play his part. To fight against Nazi Germany. He joined the Royal Armoured Corps and fought in Egypt, then up into Italy as the German army was driven north by the Allies.

His final action was as a tank driver at the Battle of Argenta Gap in April 1945, the last great battle in northern Italy. Less than a month after he took part in that, Nazi Germany had surrendered.

After all that, Tom Finney played for the England team from 1945 to 1958, earning 76 caps. When he scored his 30th international goal against Northern Ireland in October 1958, he became, at that time, England's leading scorer.

In 1998 he was knighted and became Sir Tom Finney, who had been a plumber from Preston, one of the great England footballers and a man who helped defeat Nazi Germany.

FRANK SOO

1942

Any England games played during the Second World War were considered unofficial internationals and therefore players who took part did not earn a cap.

A cap is what is awarded to a player who represents their country. It is an actual cap. The kind schoolboys or cubs used to wear – and sometimes still do.

Frank Soo was one of several footballers who missed out on being recorded as an official England player. Even so, he remains the first man of East Asian heritage to have worn the three lions on his chest.

Frank established himself as a Stoke City player, playing in midfield alongside Stanley Matthews. He also appeared as a guest player for Newcastle, Blackburn and Everton amongst others.

During the war he remained in the UK working in the engineering department at Michelin Tyres before being recruited in 1941 by the Royal Air Force to train flight crews.

He played nine times for England, making his debut against Wales in May 1942. Other England legends who played with him – including Stan Mortensen and Stanley Matthews – described him as elegant, intelligent and a great passer of the ball.

In the autumn of 2025, he was awarded a posthumous England cap to mark his role as a trailblazer for East and South-East Asian communities in Britain.

Sadly, like Plymouth's Jack Leslie before him, Soo never received that acknowledgment during his lifetime. He died in 1991.

AFTER THE WAR

1946

England's first game after the Second World War – like their first official game after the First World War – took place in Belfast. And – in a similar fashion to 1919 – England took the lead in the first minute, putting the thought of war behind them.

If only for a moment.

This was the first game in the 1946–47 Home Championships tournament that England would win, beating Ireland and Wales and drawing with Scotland.

Men on the England team were used to travelling over the sea and many had only recently returned from battlefields across the world, including Africa, the Alps, the Mediterranean and beyond. All aware that some didn't make it back.

The scorer of the first goal was Derby County's Raich Carter, who would later go on to manage Leeds

United. He was joined on the scoresheet by three England legends: Wilf Mannion, Tom Finney and Tommy Lawton.

The game ended Northern Ireland 2 England 7. And for the 57,011 fans in the stadium, it must have felt wonderful. The war was over. Football was back.

And for one player that day it must have felt especially good. Wilf Mannion, scorer of a hat-trick.

WILF MANNION

1946

When Wilf Mannion scored a hat-trick on his England
debut in 1946, he was united with other players and
tens of thousands of fans at Windsor Park in Belfast
in getting back to celebrating what they loved
about life.

Football.

Mannion had suspended his football career for
Middlesbrough to join the British Army Expeditionary
Force in 1940, an attempt to tackle the Nazi advance
across Europe. Fighting in France he was reported
killed in the local newspapers, but it later transpired
that he was one of the 200,000 people rescued at
Dunkirk in that famous retreat on little ships across
the English Channel.

Mannion also fought in Egypt, and took part in
the invasion of Sicily, part of the Allied forces sent to

overthrow Benito Mussolini, who, an ally of Hitler, was still in power in Italy.

The battles he participated in were deadly and – although he came home – tens of thousands of men did not.

And then, after all that, he was selected to play for his country and became the only player in the last century to score a hat-trick on his England debut.

Wilf Mannion went on to score 11 goals in 26 games for England. That tally included a World Cup finals goal against Chile in 1950.

He is considered Middlesbrough's greatest player and a statue of him stands outside their Riverside Stadium.

1946

Len Shackleton was capped only five times for England, with his first cap coming in the first game after the Second World War.

His five appearances spanned six years. There was a reason for that.

Shackleton was an entertainer, but he was trouble, too. He was rebellious. He challenged authority. And it cost him.

When one of the England selectors was asked why he was not chosen more often to represent his country, he said they were playing at Wembley, not the London Palladium.

The London Palladium was a theatre. The selector was suggesting that Shackleton was a showman, a showboater, a show-off. And it was true he had a nickname: The Clown Prince of Football.

So, even though he scored 127 goals as a left-sided forward in 384 games for Bradford Park Avenue, Newcastle and Sunderland, he only played the five times for England.

During the war Shackleton was conscripted to work as a miner and then in the Royal Air Force.

His final England appearance in 1954 brought his only goal. But it was a goal that sealed a 3–1 victory over West Germany in the first England game against the country they had been at war with, only a decade earlier. That must have been a meaningful day.

And the stadium?

Wembley.

1948

Tommy Lawton played for England between the ages of 19 and 28. During that period, 1938–48, he played 46 times for his country and scored 46 goals, putting him up there with the great England centre forwards, if not the greatest.

But… because he played during the war years half of his games were not counted as official internationals, so his record reads: 23 appearances, 22 goals. Still astonishing, but slightly less so.

Lawton played for England while a club player at Everton, Chelsea and Notts County. A classic centre forward, his stats and records are amazing.

When he made his first appearance, at age 19, he became the youngest England player to score on his debut. That feat wouldn't be surpassed until 2016 when 18-year-old Marcus Rashford scored against

Australia.

Lawton scored in his first six England games, all before his 20th birthday, and in his post-war career for the national side, he scored four goals in two separate games.

If it hadn't been for the war, Tommy Lawton would have been even more of a legend.

POST WAR

1946–1950

In the years following the Second World War,
England's men's football team achieved an amazing
series of results.

Between 28 September 1946 and 25 June 1950,
England played 30 games. All were played under
England's first official team manager, former RAF man,
Walter Winterbottom.

Although Winterbottom was allowed to coach
the team and decide matchday tactics, he could not
select the players. That was decided by a selection
committee at the FA.

Even so, this was England's remarkable record
over those first 30 post-war games:

Won	23
Drawn	3
Lost	4

| Goals for | 102 |
| Goals against | 30 |

This run included several massive victories, over the following:

Switzerland	6–0
Northern Ireland	7–2
Netherlands	8–2
Northern Ireland	9–2
Portugal	10–0

England were in strong form as the 1940s ended. And now, as the 1950s were about to begin, they were about to compete in their first World Cup.

ENGLAND'S FIRST QUALIFIER

1950

To reach their first World Cup finals – Rio de Janeiro, Brazil 1950 – England had to qualify. A one-off knockout game.

You would hope for an easy passage. But no.

What could be more difficult than having to go to Hampden Park in Glasgow needing to win against Scotland? And in front of 133,250 largely hostile fans.

England faced a tough assignment on that Saturday, 15 April 1950. Only one team from Britain could go to Brazil. And it was going to be Scotland or England.

If you watch the footage of the game on YouTube, you can see how Scotland attacked in wave after wave, but could not find their way past England and Wolves keeper, Bert Williams.

Goalless at half-time.

But then, out of the blue, 52 minutes in, England

scored – Stan Mortensen from close range. But he was offside!

Still 0–0, England came again on 64 minutes. They had a taste for goal now, a hunger. Bobby Langton tore up the wing and Ray Bentley was in... one touch to take him between the two Scottish defenders and he blasted it into the net.

Scotland 0 England 1.

Scotland needed a draw to go to Brazil and their first World Cup. When they hit the bar late on, the team from north of the border realised it was one of those 'nearly' days, the first of many to come. Scotland would not go to Brazil to play in the World Cup finals.

But England would.

And at right back that day for England – in that first-ever World Cup qualifier – was a defender who was learning about knockout football. His name was Alf Ramsey.

You'll meet him again in 1966.

BRAZIL 1950

1950

England's first ever World Cup finals game was against Chile. It was 25 June 1950, at the Maracanã, the legendary stadium in Rio de Janeiro.

England had never played in the World Cup finals before, missing 1930, 1934 and 1938. None of the British teams had. There was an idea that British football and its home international tournament was so good that the Brits didn't need to enter this other supposedly inferior international tournament called the World Cup.

The Chile group match was not a great game. Match reports give it a low rating. It was played in driving rain, but it was hot and humid. Conditions drained the players so much that, at half-time, England players wore oxygen masks.

England scored their goals before and after half-time. Mortensen heading home from a Mullen cross on 39. Mannion shooting home after a ball from Tom Finney on 51.

The final score was 2–0. But had England proved their superiority?

Not quite.

The chance to do that would come in their second-ever World Cup finals game. Against the unfancied United States of America.

Yet England lost 1–0. Let's move on.

THE LION OF VIENNA

1952

By 1952 Austria were considered the strongest football team in Europe with recent victories including 6–0 against Ireland and an 8–1 away win to Belgium.

Meanwhile, after England's dismal 1950 World Cup finals performance, the view of British football had shifted.

If the United States could beat England, anyone could.

And before England's game against Austria on 25 May 1952 most people expected England would be beaten.

There were thousands of British soldiers in the crowd, regardless. Men who were stationed in Germany and Austria after the end of the Second World War to help keep order and to be there for security, as the Cold War with the Soviet Union was beginning to freeze relations with the West.

Nat Lofthouse, the Bolton Wanderers centre forward, was keen to reassert the good reputation of English football. He scored his first goal on 27 minutes.

Austria replied with a penalty a minute later.

After a goal from Jackie Sewell and second Austrian equaliser the score was 2–2 at half-time.

It was tight. It was tense. It was terrific.

But it took until the 83rd minute for the game to be decided.

Bert Williams, the England keeper, cleared the ball and it reached Nat Lofthouse, who ran at it hard and clipped it home. As he did so Lofthouse collided with the keeper and was knocked unconscious.

He came round to be told he'd scored and been carried off the pitch. England were winning 3–2 against the mighty Austrians. Groggily, Lofthouse insisted on playing the last five minutes.

When the final whistle went, Lofthouse was carried off the pitch a second time – this time by hundreds of British soldiers, who named him 'the Lion of Vienna'.

ROYAL REVENGE

1953

On Monday, 8 June 1953, England travelled to New York to play the United States of America in a match to celebrate the Coronation of Queen Elizabeth II. She had become Queen the previous year and would reign for 70 years. On her death, in 2022, she would be succeeded by King Charles III.

The game was regarded as a celebration, but for England captain, Billy Wright, it was a chance to put things right. He wanted revenge for the 1–0 defeat to the USA in the 1950 World Cup finals, a result that had haunted him and the English game ever since.

England were playing under floodlights for the first time, and with half-time looming, the game was triggering bad memories. England had dominated, and were the far superior team, but they were missing chance after chance. And it was still 0–0.

Could England be about to relive their worst nightmare?

The answer was no. The Broadis-Finney-Lofthouse trio was taking control.

Tom Finney played the ball to Ivor Broadis, who hooked the ball home. 1–0!

Then Lofthouse passed to Finney who struck home. 2–0!

And then – completing a thrilling 12 minutes of dominance, Broadis played Lofthouse in for a third. Three goals, either side of half-time.

The game finished 6–3 to England. Revenge was secured. The new Queen was honoured with a victory. And Billy Wright left the pitch with a broad grin.

Yet, even after this, and even after England's next three games against the USA – with wins of 8–1 (in 1959), 10–0 (in 1964) and 5–0 (in 1985) – their 1–0 defeat at Brazil 1950 would never quite be forgotten.

1953 and 1954

England played Hungary twice within the space of six months in 1953 and 1954. In doing so they suffered their two heaviest defeats since 1907.

A 6–3 leathering in London.

A 7–1 battering in Budapest.

Two teenage brothers watched the London game. Jack and Bobby Charlton.

They both understood what these defeats meant. Bobby said later that it changed his idea of football. Jack added that it was a defining moment for football in England.

It was brutal. Until those games some people still believed that England were the greatest team in the world. Not anymore.

There were several reasons for the defeats, including:

Preparation. The Hungarians trained with the ball, focusing on passing, whereas England's priority lay in fitness and strength.

Tactics. Hungary had developed a way of playing the game that they practised over and over, which included a focus on possession.

Scouting. Hungary knew how England would play. England had not even watched the Hungarians, so did not understand how good they were.

Indeed, Hungary had the better players. At the hub of everything they did was Ferenc Puskás, one of the greatest ever, who orchestrated both hammerings.

So... how could two heavy defeats go down in history as a great moment for English football?

Because – if you learn why you have lost, defeat leads to change. And those two teenagers who were watching closely, Jack Charlton and brother Bobby, would go on to lift the World Cup 12 years later.

1954

In their first game since the 6–3 hammering at the hands of Hungary at Wembley, England needed to beat Scotland to reach the 1954 World Cup finals.

Confidence must have been shaky. How do you respond to your first defeat to a foreign side at Wembley? And which was such a brutal takedown of the English game?

After just seven minutes against Scotland, England were 1–0 down. Was this going to be another horror show?

That must have been what the Scottish fans, most of the 134,554 crowd, were hoping: that their team would qualify for the World Cup tournament at their great rival's expense.

But this was a different England team. Only three players remained in the side after the Hungary horror show: Billy Wright, Tom Finney and Ivor Broadis. Four players were making their debut for England.

And the opposition, reasoned England, was one they knew well. This was Scotland, not Hungary.

On 14 minutes England equalised Scotland's opener.

The half-time score was 1–1. That place in the 1954 World Cup finals was within England's grasp.

The second half was an aerial masterclass from England. Headers from Johnny Nicholls, Ronnie Allen and Jimmy Mullen which shocked the Scots.

And, although the Scots scored once more, the game ended Scotland 2 England 4.

England were heading to the World Cup finals. Again.

SWITZERLAND 1954

1954

England travelled to Switzerland for their second World Cup finals with the hope of performing so well that they could forget what had happened in Rio at Brazil 1950. That 1–0 defeat to the United States was still hard to forget.

There was a big doubt hanging over the team. After those heavy defeats against Hungary, could England even get out of the group stages?

They started well. Against Belgium in their first group game, they were 3–1 up with under 20 minutes to go – but they ended up drawing 4–4. Two goals from Lofthouse, and one each from Finney and Broadis, showed England were strong up front. Their weakness lay in their defence.

Hope came from a clean sheet after a 2–0 win in the second group game against the hosts, Switzerland.

With goals again from James Mullen and Dennis Wilshaw.

Then England were into the knockout stages, and a quarter-final facing the holders of the World Cup. The exceptional Uruguayans who had won the 1950 tournament in the Maracanã Stadium against hosts and favourites, Brazil. Uruguay – a team who had, in the 1954 group stages, beaten Scotland 7–0.

But England would suffer a 4–2 defeat to Uruguay. Not even goals from the reliable Lofthouse and Finney could overcome the two-time winners of the Jules Rimet Trophy.

England came away with the newspapers and television reporting that they had done well. Games against the World Cup hosts and the World Cup holders are never easy, but a defeat is a defeat and England were out.

DUNCAN EDWARDS

1956

England's 3–1 win in Berlin in a 1956 friendly is remembered not because it was a rare win away in West Germany, but for the goal that Duncan Edwards scored. It was how the England midfielder announced himself as potentially one of the world's great players.

A Manchester United player, Edwards was considered the all-round footballer. He was tall and strong. He had such power and presence that he made his debut for United aged just 16. He was famous for covering practically every blade of grass on the pitch when he played. He went on to help his club win two league titles.

Edwards's goal against West Germany came on 25 minutes.

The ball spun loose halfway into the West Germany half. With his back to goal, Edwards took control, leaping over a German player on the floor, then turning with the ball close to his feet and dribbling between two German defenders. Three touches. That third touch created a yard of space for him in front of the oncoming defender. Whereupon Edwards blasted the ball home.

Duncan Edwards was still a teenager when he scored this goal.

Yet just two years later he was dead. One of eight Manchester United players to be killed in the 1958 Munich Air Disaster.

1957

Stanley Matthews was the son of a boxer. As a result, he knew how to keep himself fighting fit. But, unlike his dad, he did his fighting on the football pitch, not in the ring.

Matthews is – and will probably always be – the oldest man to play football for England. He made his debut when he was 19, and his last game for England came when he was 42.

Bear in mind most footballers don't make it past 35. And that is just for their clubs, not their countries. Only six England players have ever played into their 40th year. Five were goalkeepers. The other – and only outfield player – was Matthews.

Stanley Matthews was an absolute legend. He was one of the first footballers to enter the FA Hall of Fame. The first to win the Ballon D'Or. His dribbling skills along with his vision for a killer pass caused the 1953 FA Cup Final to be named the Matthews Final.

Matthews's last game for England was a World Cup qualifier in Denmark in 1957. It was a 4–1 win that all but ensured that England would qualify for the 1958 World Cup.

Matthews was done at international level. He carried on playing as a professional at club level into his early fifties.

In 1965, the year he retired from club football, he was knighted, becoming Sir Stanley Matthews.

1958

Just four months after the Munich Air Disaster, England travelled to Sweden for their third appearance in the World Cup finals.

England were drawn in a group with the Soviet Union, Brazil and Austria. All three matches ended level. So, England and the Soviet Union – both on three points from three games – were required to play off for a place in the quarter-finals.

England were on top in the playoff. Creating chance after chance and plenty of shots on goal. It was one of those games where if you take your chances, you can win 2–0 or 3–0.

But England had come up against the greatest goalie of all time.

Just as the Soviet Union became involved in a space race against the USA, with each superpower putting satellites into space, the Soviets' Russian keeper, Lev Yashin, became an icon of football.

Yashin – the man who revolutionised goalkeeping – made a number of reflex saves, collecting one ball after England had hit the post. England even had a goal disallowed for handball.

And then – after all the pressure from England – the Soviet Union went up to the other end of the pitch and scored.

That's knockout football. England were out.

But bear something in mind…

Due to the Munich Air Disaster of February 1958, England had lost at least four players who would probably have been in that World Cup finals squad, if not the team that day. Manchester United had been champions of England in 1956 and 1957, and Roger Byrne, David Pegg, Tommy Taylor and Duncan Edwards had all played for England before losing their lives in the air crash.

1959

Billy Wright made his England debut in 1946. His final game – and 90th as captain – came as the 1950s came to an end, and against his 'nightmare' team, the United States.

It was 1959, and the world was looking to the future now, not back to the twentieth century's two world wars.

But England were still haunted by that 1–0 World Cup defeat to the USA in 1950. It had been the lowest low England had suffered and now, nine years later, after 18 minutes, Billy Wright might have been thinking he was captaining England to another embarrassment.

Because USA were leading England 1–0. The home crowd were going wild at the thought of once more humiliating the English at their own sport.

But the Americans were to be disappointed. By the end of the game, Billy Wright had led his men to an 8–1 victory. His time as captain and England legend was over, and he ended his run in style.

As part of that England victory, incidentally, was a hat-trick from the promising Bobby Charlton, then 21 years old. The 1960s, England's greatest footballing decade, was on the horizon.

HOSTING THE WORLD CUP

1960

Who should host the World Cup finals is decided by a vote. Members of FIFA each vote to select which of the bids from interested countries is the best.

Three countries bid for the 1966 World Cup: England. Spain. West Germany.

The vote took place in August 1960.

At the last minute – seeing that they were probably going to come last – Spain withdrew and supported the West German bid.

They made a deal that if Spain supported West Germany's bid for 1966, West Germany would support Spain in 1974.

But that still didn't work.

The final score was:

England 34 West Germany 27.

And so, England would host the FIFA World Cup in 1966.

STRATOSPHERIC

1961

England's biggest ever victory over Scotland came in the British Home Internationals in April 1961.

At the time, the Russian cosmonaut Yuri Gagarin was in all the newspapers, and would go down in history for having just survived man's first flight in space. Elvis Presley was the biggest popular music star, with a string of number one hits.

And the young Queen, Elizabeth II, was present at Wembley Stadium and ready to present the Home International trophy to England. But only if England could avoid defeat. A draw would do.

The final score was:

England 9 Scotland 3.

It was England's captain, Johnny Haynes, who orchestrated the destruction of their oldest rivals.

First on the score sheet was Bobby Robson, running

onto a pass from Jimmy Greaves to thump the ball home. You'll meet Bobby Robson again later when in 1990, as manager, he guides England to a World Cup semi-final.

Jimmy Greaves went on to complete a hat-trick that day. He would score 44 goals in his 57 appearances for his country.

But the performance of the day came from Johnny Haynes (scorer of two goals) who collected the Home International trophy from the Queen after climbing the famous steps at Wembley.

1962

England reached the quarter-finals of the 1962 World Cup. It was their joint best performance so far, having reached the same stage in 1954.

After losing to Hungary in the first game in Group 4, they beat Argentina and drew with Bulgaria to finish second in the group.

But a quarter-final against Brazil, both holders of 1958's World Cup and ultimately 1962's winners, was a bridge too far for England. They lost 3–1.

One highlight of 1962, though, was England's Jimmy Armfield being named the best right-back in the world by legend of legends, Pelé. Before the game, the Brazilian noted, Bobby Charlton was the talk of everyone in Brazil, but afterwards, all the attention was on Armfield.

Jimmy Armfield was a one-club player, turning

out for Blackpool hundreds of times. He went on to become a successful manager, taking Leeds United to the final of the 1975 European Cup, only to be cheated out of the victory by a corrupt referee. He played 43 times for England.

In 1962, England had gone through another World Cup disappointment – albeit at the hands of the greatest football team to ever exist – but maybe the next World Cup tournament, to take place in England itself, in 1966, would bring better results.

ALF RAMSEY

1962

In October 1962, Alfred Ernest Ramsey was named England manager, replacing Walter Winterbottom who had done the job since the end of the Second World War. Ramsey would not take up the role until May 1963, though, as he wanted to honour his contract as Ipswich Town manager.

He was like that, Alf. He wanted to do things the right way. He'd been in the Army during the Second World War and knew that things had to be done properly.

But, saying that, if he saw something that needed changing, Alf would change it. And he saw things that needed changing in the England set-up. The changes he made would ensure that he became considered the first proper England manager.

How did he do this?

It was simple. He insisted that he should pick the team.

Up until then a selection committee at the FA had selected the teams. But that wouldn't work for Alf. The England players were his players. Like his players at Ipswich Town had been his players when they won the league in 1962.

Anyone playing for England now would know that Alf had chosen them. They would play for him and not some distant board of suits in a room.

His next act as England manager was to select Bobby Moore as his captain.

1963

England travelled to Europe in May 1963 to play three games on an end-of-season European tour. They would face East Germany and Switzerland. But first, they visited the country that had lost to Brazil in the 1962 World Cup final: Czechoslovakia.

Two out of their three games were in Eastern Europe, an area that had become dominated by the Soviet Union after the Second World War, as part of the Cold War between the West and the East.

The game was notable for one more reason. It would be the first with Bobby Moore as captain of England. His spell as captain, succeeding that of Johnny Haynes, would last for over a decade, and include both the 1966 and 1970 World Cup tournaments.

Moore was 22 years old. The youngest England

captain. And a record that still stands.

With a new manager and a new captain, England played bravely, soaking up the inevitable Czech pressure, then striking on the break. It was a tactical masterclass from Alf Ramsey. A new England.

England won 4–2 with goals from Bobby Charlton, Bobby Smith and two from Jimmy Greaves.

The sort of names that would fill the history books for the next decade in the English game.

Ramsey. Charlton. Greaves.

And England's captain, Moore.

WE WILL WIN IT

1963

Not long after he became England manager, Alf Ramsey made what many people thought was a bizarre prediction.

He believed that England would win the World Cup in 1966.

Some people laughed at him. Openly mocked him. This quietly spoken man, who rarely smiled, saying something like that.

After all, in their four World Cup tournaments so far, England had only ever qualified for the quarter-finals. They were famous for their arrogant assumption that they were the best in the world. But they were not.

Not yet.

But there was some logic in what Alf Ramsey said that day about winning it. England would be the hosts of 1966. That gave them home advantage. And the players coming through were an exceptional group: Moore. Greaves. Jack and Bobby Charlton. Goalkeeper Gordon Banks.

It could happen. Couldn't it?

Either way, by saying it, Alf Ramsey was manifesting the greatest moment in the history of the English game.

PICKLES

1966

In the run-up to England 1966, the English Football Association put the then World Cup trophy on display. They did this to build up excitement about the forthcoming tournament.

But, while the security guards looking after the Jules Rimet Trophy were on a break, it was stolen.

The thieves sent the Football Association a ransom note, demanding £15,000 for the return of the trophy. (That's about £400,000 in today's money.)

Before the ransom money was paid, a man called Dave took his dog, Pickles, for a walk. Dave needed to use a phone booth to make a call. This was a time when many people didn't even have phones in their homes, let alone in their pockets.

En route, Pickles started sniffing around under

some bushes, round the back of a car and he found something.

A parcel.

And inside the parcel?

The Jules Rimet Trophy.

Dave and his dog were national heroes. Pickles received awards, including Dog of the Year.

Some people claimed the whole story – the theft and the dog finding the trophy – was a publicity stunt so that more people would buy tickets for the games. Who knows? It was probably real.

ENGLAND 1966

1966

The host nation, England were drawn against Uruguay, Mexico and France in Group 1 of the World Cup finals.

The first game, against Uruguay, was a bore draw. A 0–0 in which, however much England tried to deploy their dangerous attacking trio – Roger Hunt, Bobby Charlton and Jimmy Greaves – they could not find a way through in front of 90,000 passionate England fans at Wembley.

A frustrating start. The Uruguayans celebrated the draw as if they had won the World Cup, for a third time.

England moved on. Their next game was Mexico. Wembley again.

As half-time approached it was 0–0. The fans were becoming restless. And then Bobby Charlton picked up the ball and ran with it. A direct line to the edge of the penalty area where he hit it. Hard.

It was 1–0 to England.

That was more like it.

In the second half Roger Hunt of Liverpool scored, poaching a goal after the Mexican keeper couldn't hold onto a save.

England 2 Mexico 0.

In their third game, England had to beat France to top their group. They proceeded to do just that – Hunt tapping in after Jack Charlton headed an effort off the post. Then, a second goal from Hunt.

So, England topped Group 1 and qualified for the knockout stages of the tournament. They had scored four goals and conceded none. The only team who had not yet let in a goal.

Next up, Argentina.

And trouble...

ANIMALS

1966

After the England-Argentina quarter-final in the 1966 World Cup, the England manager, Alf Ramsey, stopped his players changing shirts with the Argentina team.

He described the opposition as 'animals', and wanted his side to have nothing to do with them.

It had been a brutal game. Fouls from both sides, but mostly from Argentina, whose captain, Antonio Rattín, contested every decision. Bullying the referee, or at least trying to.

And so... he was sent off. For a while Rattín refused to leave the pitch and, after several minutes, the police finally led the Argentina captain away.

The match is also notable as the only time Bobby Charlton was booked while playing for England. His brother, Jack, had gone down with an Argentina player and, on the ground, was being kicked and stood on.

Bobby ran over and pushed the opposition players away from Jack. The referee took his name.

England won the tie 1–0 with a perfectly timed header from Geoff Hurst, who stole the show. The first of his four goals in the tournament. You might know when he would score his other three…

The Argentinians have described the game with the phrase 'the robbery of the century' – a shame, as they were a very gifted team and could have shown that instead of behaving like 'animals'.

1966

England have appeared in three World Cup semi-finals. The first was against Portugal in 1966. It remains the only one they have won.

England were up against one of the world's greatest ever players, Eusébio, who had already scored seven goals in the tournament. He was a powerful, accurate, skilful player, who had claimed four in Portugal's quarter-final, where at one stage they were trailing North Korea by 3–0.

But it was Bobby Charlton's goal-scoring that made the headlines in that day's semi-final.

Charlton created two powerful shots (in the 31st and 73rd minutes) from the edge of the area, although he was so good, he made the shots look like passes into the back of the net.

Portugal did not give up. They attacked relentlessly.

This was a World Cup semi-final. There were 17 minutes to go.

After 83 minutes, a Portugal shot from the left of the penalty area was going in. Two hands reached up to stop the ball reaching goal. Jack Charlton and Nobby Stiles had both handled it.

Although an intentional handball was a foul, it didn't lead to an automatic sending off until 1990. You would be booked, but not sent off. So, Jack Charlton, the first to handle it, was booked.

A penalty for Portugal. Eusébio stepped up. And he scored.

The Portuguese international grabbed the ball and ran back for the kick-off.

Eusébio would end the tournament as leading scorer with eight goals. But there was no time for him to score a ninth. At the final whistle he broke down in tears. It had been his last chance to carry Portugal to their first World Cup final. Instead, England would face West Germany.

WORLD CUP FINAL: THE ENGLAND TEAM

1966

When most of Britain sat down to watch the 1966 World Cup final, they would watch it in black and white. Colour TV did not exist at all in Britain until 1967 (on BBC2), and even then, colour sets were expensive. There were only three TV channels at that time: BBC1, BBC2 and ITV. And, of course, there was no internet.

Whether people watched the game at home – if they owned or rented a TV set – or in cinemas and halls, one thing was certain: they were watching the greatest moment in the history of the English game.

This is the England team (listed with the clubs they played for) that played throughout normal and extra time on that historic day, 30 July, in the 1966 World Cup final:

1	Gordon Banks	Leicester City
2	George Cohen	Fulham
3	Ray Wilson	Everton
4	Nobby Stiles	Manchester United
5	Jack Charlton	Leeds United
6	Bobby Moore	West Ham United
7	Alan Ball	Blackpool
16	Martin Peters	West Ham United
9	Bobby Charlton	Manchester United
10	Geoff Hurst	West Ham United
21	Roger Hunt	Liverpool

1966

The score of the 1966 World Cup final, at the end of normal time, was 2–2.

West Germany had scored after 12 minutes, but Hurst (in the 18th minute) and Peters (in the 78th) ensured that England were 2–1 up, with just a minute to go. Fans were already celebrating around the country, but it was premature.

The Germans equalised right at the death.

And so… to extra time.

That West Germany equaliser led to one of the most controversial moments in the history of England football.

A controversial moment, but a good moment. If you're English:

Eleven minutes into the first half of extra time, Alan Ball ran down the wing. He crossed to Geoff

Hurst. Hurst had his back to the goal, a few yards out, but – unchallenged and having skilfully created the space for himself – he controlled the ball, turned, and shot.

Hurst's shot hit the crossbar and crashed down close to the goal-line.

England celebrated. The Germans objected. The referee ran over to the linesman, a former player from Azerbaijan. After a brief discussion, Tofiq Bahramov confirmed the ball crossed the line.

It was a goal. According to the 'Russian linesman'.

Was it a goal? You decide…

But either way, England were 3–2 ahead.

THEY THINK IT'S ALL OVER

1966

And here comes Hurst.
He's got…
Some people are on the pitch.
They think it's all over…
It is now.

This famous commentary on England's fourth goal in the 1966 World Cup final came from Kenneth Wolstenholme.

It was the last minute of extra time. England led 3–2. West Germany were throwing everything at the England defence, desperate to score another late, late equaliser…

The ball was played out of the England half. A long ball from England captain, Bobby Moore. Most of the West Germany players were still up field. Defenders included.

Geoff Hurst collected the ball, touched it one, two, three, four times, towards the German goal. An army of German defenders were sprinting back to catch Hurst.

The German keeper tried to narrow his angles. And now a defender was gaining on Hurst.

But, cool under pressure, Hurst smashed the ball into the net for his hat-trick.

4–2.

England had won the World Cup.

GENTLEMAN BOBBY MOORE

1966

When Bobby Moore walked up the Wembley steps to collect the Jules Rimet trophy, he noticed that Queen Elizabeth II, who was there to present the trophy, was wearing long white gloves.

Moore, as England captain, was about to shake hands with her and receive the World Cup.

The TV footage of this moment is incredible.

First, Moore looked at his right hand. Then he subtly wiped both his hands on his white shorts, then again on his red top, and then finally on the gantry in front of him. To free them from the mud and sweat of 120 minutes of football.

Only now did Bobby Moore take the hand of the Queen, shaking it gently, and dipping his head in deference.

Moore never spoke of his gesture. But it is reported

the Queen noticed and was very impressed.

Jack Charlton, defender on the day, commented on Moore's thoughtfulness, and described the rest of the team, himself included, as looking like they had just been down a coalmine.

From the opposition, West Germany's Franz Beckenbauer believed that Moore's gesture was the mark of a true gentleman.

Euro 68

England's first European Championship finals came in 1968, as they had not entered the inaugural 1960 tournament, and had failed to qualify in 1964.

The Euros were a different beast in those days. Only four teams qualified to take part: in 1968, they were Italy (the hosts), the Soviet Union, Yugoslavia and England.

The Italy-Soviet semi-final ended in a draw and was decided... by the toss of a coin. Italy won that.

England lost their semi-final 1–0 to Yugoslavia but went on to play the Soviet Union for what was called the bronze medal. A third-place play-off – like we still have in the World Cup finals.

The England-Soviet play-off was decided by two goals. One in the first half – Bobby Charlton leathering the ball past the Soviet keeper from eight yards.

Another in the second half – from 1966 hat-trick hero, Geoff Hurst, who exploited a mistake from the Soviet keeper.

The final between Italy and Yugoslavia ended in a draw, so, two days later, they replayed the final.

All this feels old fashioned now. Replayed finals. Bronze medals. Only four teams – not 24 – in the finals. That's how it was then.

But deciding a semi-final on the toss of a coin? That's bizarre, isn't it?

At least it was the Soviet Union and not England who had to suffer that.

THE BOGOTÁ BRACELET

1970

The period leading up to the 1970 World Cup in Mexico was the strangest of times. Man had set foot on the Moon less than a year before. To people then, that event was like something out of a sci-fi movie.

In addition, a war that wasn't a war was being fought: the Cold War between the West and Russia.

In the world of football itself, Bobby Moore, the man who had shown such respect to Queen Elizabeth II in 1966, became a most unlikely suspect four years later. In the days leading up to the 1970 World Cup tournament, he was arrested for stealing a bracelet in Bogotá, Colombia.

A shop assistant at the jewellers in the team's hotel said she had witnessed Moore take the bracelet. Another woman claimed she had seen the theft through the window.

Moore denied it vehemently – and it turned out that the jewellery store was trying to get money out of famous faces visiting their shop. It was a nasty trick.

The England captain was cleared of any wrongdoing. He went on to play superbly in the 1970 World Cup finals, though England were beaten 3–2 by West Germany in the quarter-finals.

1970

England drew Brazil in the group stages of the 1970 World Cup finals in Mexico. A tough opponent and the team who would go on to win the trophy.

The game offered up what many believe to be the greatest save of all time:

Ten minutes in, Jairzinho powers down the right wing and fires a perfect deep cross to Pelé, eight yards out. The Brazilian Number 9 heads the ball into the ground in front of England keeper, Gordon Banks.

Pelé puts his arms in the air and shouts, 'Goal!'

But Banks has dived down to his right and – somehow – has got a hand to the ball, has resisted the power of Pelé's header and has forced the ball up the eight-foot height of the goal and over the bar.

It is the most extraordinary save.

Later in the game, Banks was beaten via a goal

from Jairzinho, and England lost 1–0. But Banks's save is the true legacy of that game.

Pelé subsequently joked that he had scored over 1,000 goals in his career, but all everyone wanted to discuss with him was the goal he didn't score. The header saved by England's Gordon Banks.

As previously mentioned, England went out of the 1970 World Cup in the quarter-finals. They would not play in the finals again until 12 years later in 1982, missing Germany 1974 and Argentina 1978. Nor did they qualify for either of the 1970s' Euro championships in 1972 or 1976.

MOORE 90

In November 1973, Bobby Moore equalled his hero, Billy Wright's record of captaining England the most times.

The game was Moore's last as captain and last for England. It came in a 1–0 defeat to Italy at Wembley.

Bobby Moore saw Billy Wright as a role model, a hero. He admired his style as a captain and footballer – plus his calmness under pressure, his sportsmanship and his leading by example.

Moore and Wright remain those who have captained England the most times.

Ninety.

That record will probably be broken in 2026 – by Harry Kane. Can he do what Bobby Moore did and lift the World Cup trophy?

A footnote… On the Italian side that day of

Moore's last game in 1973, there was a midfielder called Fabio Capello. He scored the winner. He would return to Wembley in 2007 – as manager of England.

Super League Cup 1986

After England didn't qualify for the 1974 World Cup under Sir Alf Ramsey, they had three managers in the space of four years. First came Joe Mercer. Then came Don Revie, under whom England failed to qualify for Euro 1976 in Yugoslavia.

It was left to Revie's successor as manager, Ron Greenwood, to get England back into tournament football.

To qualify for the World Cup finals 1978 in Argentina, England were drawn in a tough group, against Italy, Finland and Luxembourg. Tough because Italy was one of the best teams in the world at that time.

Losing to Italy 2–0 in November 1976, England had to win the second leg at home a year later to have a chance of reaching the finals in Argentina.

And they did. With Kevin Keegan at the centre of everything.

Keegan, then a young emerging forward from Yorkshire, scored the first goal from a Trevor Brooking cross and returned the favour by playing in Brooking to England's second.

The Italians feared Keegan. At one point Keegan was elbowed in the face by legendary Italian defender, Marco Tardelli. Later Keegan was fouled again and pushed Tardelli back. It was Keegan who was booked.

Italy had to beat Luxembourg in the final group game to finish above England on goal difference.

They did. But not before Keegan had rattled them at Wembley.

And – even though they failed again to reach the finals of a tournament – England had still shown their potential remained, to play on the world stage.

1978

For many years, since his debut in 1978, Viv Anderson was acknowledged as the first Black player – or person of colour – who appeared as a full senior international for England.

Anderson was a superb defender, who spent his best years as part of Brian Clough's astonishing Nottingham Forest team of the late 1970s and early 1980s.

He made his England debut against Czechoslovakia and went on to represent his country 30 times, scoring twice.

Though Anderson is often credited as the first of many Black men to pull on the white shirt, it belies the contributions of earlier figures.

We have already seen the disappointing treatment given to Plymouth's Jack Leslie in 1925, whose invitation to play for England was withdrawn. Many point out that the first non-white player to actually play for England was Frank Soo, who had Chinese heritage, during the years of the Second World War. There was also the mixed-race Leeds United legend Paul Reaney, whose first of three caps representing England came when he appeared as a substitute against Bulgaria in 1968.

Either way, Anderson, Soo and Reaney (plus the marginalised Jack Leslie) were all pioneers for the many players from the diverse communities of England who have worn three lions on their shirts.

EURO 80

1980

Having not qualified for the last four major football tournaments of the 1970s, England were back. It had been a long wait, but they began the 1980 European Championship finals in spectacular style. Drawn in the toughest of groups against Belgium, Spain and the host nation, Italy, England drew first blood:

Against Belgium, 26 minutes in, Ray Wilkins collected a loose clearance. He was 25 yards out. He needed one touch to control it, then, under pressure on the edge of the area, he lofted the ball over two oncoming defenders, kept running and was in the clear, one on one with the Belgian keeper. He waited for the ball to fall. The keeper squatted, expecting a low shot, but Wilkins surprised everyone, lobbing it over him and into the net.

England led 1–0. What a start.

But that's when it all began to go wrong.

Belgium equalised three minutes later, and goaded by Italian fans in the stadium, the England fans attacked back. The Italian police used tear gas to combat the trouble, and the game had to be suspended for a few minutes as players were affected by the gas, notably England's goalkeeper, Ray Clemence.

A shameful day for England.

And Ray Wilkins's beautiful goal was forgotten.

1981

It was 11 years since England last qualified for the World Cup finals. In the group stages for Spain 1982, they had one last chance to qualify. They had to avoid defeat against Hungary at Wembley.

But Hungary had just hammered Norway and Switzerland to finish top of the group.

It all made for a very tense night at Wembley.

The goal that won the game for England didn't appear to be the most attractive you might see. But for those who were lucky enough to see it… it was a thing of beauty.

The Hungarian defence cleared another England free kick, with the ball ricocheting to Trevor Brooking inside the area. Brooking backed off, creating space, and then shot.

But it was a poor shot, spinning well wide. This

from the man who had scored the winner in the FA Cup final for West Ham the year before.

Yet Ipswich Town's Paul Mariner was in the path of Brooking's wayward shot, appearing to stumble onto the ball and deflect it in.

It looked like a clumsy goal. But if you study it, it is all about Paul Mariner, adjusting his feet as the ball comes at him unexpectedly. What looks clumsy – even lucky – was a piece of extraordinary skill.

And England were going to the World Cup finals for the first time in half a generation. To Spain 1982.

1982

England were in the World Cup finals for the first time since the 1970 World Cup.

England v France. In the Spanish sunshine. There was a month of football on the TV. And it was all anyone would be talking about.

The game kicked off against France, and England attacked first. Down the right. They won an early throw in. Steve Coppell took it long, a powerful throw into the French penalty area. The ball reached the head of Terry Butcher, who helped it on to Manchester United's Bryan Robson.

Robson was unmarked. Just him and the keeper. How could that be? The game was 27 seconds old!

The French keeper came out.

Robson shaped his body to half-volley the ball towards the goal.

And it was in!

It was in!

Was this real?

The commentator couldn't quite believe it either. 'What a start for England!' he shouted.

After beating France, England went on to win against Czechoslovakia and Kuwait in their group, before drawing 0–0 with both Spain and West Germany in a second group phase. This second group phase was before the creation of the Round of 16 and quarter-finals format in 1986. It was a curious format, and it punished England. They failed to reach the semi-finals.

1984

When Brazil wanted to celebrate the refurbishment and reopening of their world-famous football stadium, the Maracanã in Rio de Janeiro, and the 70th anniversary of the founding of the Brazilian Football Federation, they invited England to be their opponents.

It was a great gesture from Brazil to invite England. Although England – the founders of association football – had come from where many believed was the home of football, Wembley Stadium, many others believed that the real home of football was the Maracanã Stadium.

Why? Because football flair and excitement was Brazil's way. Players running with the ball. Exciting attacking. Outrageous skills. And – back then at least – English football was seen as dull and predictable. Long balls, bloody head wounds, hard tackles.

Just before half-time, those ideas were turned on their head when a young winger from Watford FC took up the ball. John Barnes was playing his tenth game of 79 for his country.

From close to the halfway line, Barnes picked up the ball and began a probing run, past one man, then another. Suddenly he was in the Brazil penalty area, between two Brazil defenders, and then he was beyond their keeper, so perplexed and bamboozled that he appeared to drop onto his backside. This allowed Barnes to knock the ball into the net.

It remains, arguably, England's greatest-ever goal.

Barnes, talking later in life, mused that the Brazilians didn't tackle him because they were in a state of shock. They couldn't believe an Englishman was going to do this.

But an Englishman had done it. John Barnes.

1986

For England, the World Cup in Mexico was not going well. They lost their first group match to Portugal, 1–0. In the second game, against Morocco, they not only merely drew 0–0, but were down to ten men for the second half when midfield maestro Ray Wilkins was sent off.

Now, with Wilkins consequently unavailable for the game against Poland, England manager Bobby Robson had to make some changes. England needed to beat Poland to qualify for the knockout stages.

But Poland were top of their group after beating the team who beat England: Portugal. And England hadn't scored a single goal in the tournament yet.

In Wilkins's absence, Robson chose a four-four-two formation, pinning his hopes on striker Gary Lineker.

On eight minutes, Gary Stevens crossed for Lineker to score. 1–0.

On 14 minutes, Steve Hodge crossed. Lineker slotted it in. 2–0.

On 36 minutes, it was all but game over – Lineker scored again after the Polish keeper fumbled a cross.

England were in the knockout stages of a World Cup final. On course to meet Diego Maradona and Argentina…

NOT THE HAND OF GOD

1986

In the quarter-final game at Mexico, Argentina's Diego Maradona cheated when he put the ball over the England goalkeeper, Peter Shilton, and into the back of the net.

Using his arm.

The look of outrage on Shilton's face, after the ball went in, said it all.

The so-called 'Hand of God' was not one of the greatest moments in England's footballing history. It was one of the worst.

Maradona admitted he handled the ball, and he was the one who referred to it as the Hand of God. He said that his cheat goal was revenge for Argentina's defeat in the Falklands War between the two countries in 1982, when the Argentinian dictator General Galtieri had ordered the country's troops to invade the British territory.

England lost 2–1 to Argentina that day in Mexico, and their latest World Cup adventure was over. Argentina went on to win the World Cup.

So why is this moment in this book? Does anything positive come out of the 'Hand of God' incident?

There is something. At the end of the tournament England were awarded the Fair Play award. For sporting behaviour under great pressure.

VICTORY IN BELGRADE

1987

Having only taken part in two of the seven European Championship finals so far (in 1968 and 1980), England were desperate to reach 1988's tournament in West Germany.

They were drawn in a qualification group against Northern Ireland (winning 3–0 at home and 2–0 away), Turkey (drawing 0–0 away, but stuffing Turkey 8–0 at home)… and Yugoslavia.

England had already beaten Yugoslavia 2–0 at Wembley, but an away game in Belgrade was a tough assignment. And because Yugoslavia had won all their other games, England needed to draw or win the group.

If England were defeated, they would once again fail to qualify for a major tournament, and Yugoslavia would be off to West Germany.

The game was a masterclass from manager Bobby Robson. Players of the calibre of Peter Beardsley, John Barnes, Bryan Robson and Tony Adams were in the team, and all four scored, meaning that England were 4–0 up after 25 minutes.

Qualification was secured. England had the best record of the qualifying teams, having dropped only one point in the group.

Suddenly England went from fear of failure to being one of the most fancied teams to win the Euros.

But that's where the fun would stop. In West Germany, in the 1988 Euros, England faced the Republic of Ireland, the Netherlands and the Soviet Union. They lost all three games.

1989

England gained qualification for the 1990 World Cup finals with a goalless draw away in Sweden. The point was enough for England to be confident that they would travel to Italia 90 and reach their third World Cup finals on the trot.

But the Sweden game would be remembered for the heroics of the England captain, and central defender for Scottish club Rangers, Terry Butcher. In the first minute, going up for a header, Butcher collided with a Swedish defender and received a wound that bled. And bled.

And bled.

As the game wore on – now wearing a bandage round his head – Butcher's white England top was becoming redder and redder. His face was streaming with blood.

Later, a rule was introduced that if a player is bleeding they have to go off until the bleeding stops.

But this rule did not exist in 1989.

In 1989 Butcher refused to leave the field. He was playing to get his country to the World Cup finals. He wasn't coming off. Why would he come off? Photographs of Butcher looking like something out of a horror film or disaster movie showed him as a hero.

And he was. England were heading to Italia 90.

Subsequently older and wiser – aware of how many footballers have suffered terribly from brain trauma through years of heading footballs – Terry Butcher joined the chorus of voices calling for heading to be reduced or even banned in the game of football.

NESSUN DORMA

1990

Italia 90 began for most England fans with a song. The song was called 'Nessun Dorma', which means 'none shall sleep'.

The BBC chose a recording of 'Nessun Dorma' by the Italian opera singer Luciano Pavarotti as their opening theme music for their coverage of the tournament. It is a powerful, dramatic and emotional song.

As England progressed to the semi-final of Italia 90, the song became more than a theme tune. It became an anthem. It even came close to becoming a number one hit single.

1990

England v Belgium in the 1990 World Cup finals. The winner would play Cameroon in the quarter-finals.

But it was 0–0 at full-time. And it was still 0–0 with one minute of extra time to go. It looked like it was going to be penalties. And nobody likes penalties. Especially the English, as we shall see.

One last attack in the Italian heat. England had the ball. Paul Gascoigne powered forward. Forty yards out, he was fouled by two Belgians.

Free kick. Gascoigne took it. England packed the box with six forwards. They were going for it. It was chipped into the box, volleyed, and found its mark. England had scored.

Somehow David Platt of Aston Villa, a 72nd minute substitute, had stolen in behind three Belgian defenders, with his back to goal. He turned, balletic, as the ball came over his shoulder. Then he fired it home.

An exceptional goal. The fans were out of their seats in the stadium. The nation was off its sofas at home.

England 1 Belgium 0.

The Three Lions were in the quarter-finals. Drawn to play Cameroon. A game that everyone assumed would be an easy passage to the last four.

1990

Before England played their World Cup quarter-final against Cameroon, they held an open training session for local Italians and the media to watch.

It is a thing teams do. To thank the local community for hosting them. And to allow football fans who don't have tickets for games to see famous players play.

The story goes that England manager, Bobby Robson, heard a Cameroon ally was there, watching how England trained. Spying, even. Robson warned Gary Lineker about it.

Whether there was a spy there or not, those watching would have noticed Gary Lineker take his penalties one way.

On the day of the quarter-final, England took an early lead through David Platt, a bullet header from a

Stuart Pearce cross. They led 1–0 at half-time.

But in the second half, in the space of five minutes on the hour mark, Cameroon shredded England's defence and scored twice. Suddenly England were losing to a team they were supposed to beat easily.

There were five minutes left when Lineker controlled the ball inside the penalty area. He shaped to shoot. And was brought down. Penalty!

Lineker stepped up and put it the opposite way to how he had played it in training. The keeper dived right. 2–2.

Extra time. More tension. Five minutes pass. Ten minutes. Then Lineker was in again. He was fouled again.

Another penalty. Another goal for Lineker. 3–2 to England.

England would play West Germany in the semi-final, where penalties would be an issue too…

GAZZA'S TEARS

1990

After Paul Gascoigne was booked in the 99th minute of the World Cup semi-final against West Germany, he cried.

Here was a young man who had grown up wanting to be a footballer, wanting to play for his country, wanting to play in a World Cup final. Like everyone watching had wanted when they were children.

And Gazza was doing it. Living everyone's dream.

But now he had been booked, that dream was over. He had made a clumsy tackle, and put a German down.

Because Gazza had already been booked against Belgium in the Round of 16 game, he now had two yellow cards, which meant he would miss the next game.

The World Cup final. If England qualified.

So, when Gazza cried in front of the world, everyone was with him.

And he came home a national treasure.

SUCCESS IN DEFEAT

1990

England lost their semi-final against West Germany. A 4–3 defeat in a penalty shoot-out following a 1–1 draw after extra time.

After missing his spot-kick by hitting the German keeper's legs, Stuart Pearce's face was grim as he walked back to the halfway line. Gary Lineker put a supportive arm round him.

England were out.

But the fans did not see it as a failure. Was reaching a World Cup semi-final and losing on penalties considered to be failure?

Clearly not.

When England came home, 100,000 fans were waiting at Luton Airport for them. Cheering. Chanting. Proud.

The pilot pointed out the crowds to the players as

their plane came in to land at the airport.

David Platt – who had heroically scored against Belgium – commented on how they had felt like they'd let the country down by losing. But the fans had turned out in their hundreds of thousands to tell them the opposite. It was a memory he would never forget.

PETER SHILTON

1990

Peter Shilton's last cap for England came in the third-place play-off at the end of Italia 90.

Having lost to West Germany in the semi-final, England went on to play Italy, the hosts, for third place.

Shilton retired from international football after Italia 90.

It was his 125th appearance for his country. That record still stands. Shilton is England's most capped player.

He played in three World Cup final tournaments and three European Championship final tournaments between 1980 and 1990, and could have had even more caps, had Ron Greenwood not alternated Shilton and Ray Clemence as goalkeeper during his managership.

At the time of writing, Harry Kane is on 112 appearances for England. If England reach the semi-finals of the 2026 World Cup finals, Kane will come close to matching Shilton's record.

IT'S COMING HOME

1996

In the summer of 1996, England – whose team were managed by the charismatic Terry Venables – hosted their first men's football European Championship.

Football was coming home.

There was huge excitement. Host teams often win tournaments. They certainly stand a better chance. After all, England had last hosted a major football tournament in 1966.

The excitement seemingly felt even more intense because, under previous manager Graham Taylor, England had failed to even qualify for the Euros in Sweden 1992, and at the USA 1994 World Cup finals had only scored one goal and finished bottom of their group.

So, for Euro 1996, England needed a song, an anthem, a battle cry.

Two English comedians – and football fans – David Baddiel and Frank Skinner were, at the time, hosting a TV football show called *Fantasy Football League*, and teamed up with Ian Broudie of the band The Lightning Seeds, to write and record a new song.

Incidentally, you might recognise David Baddiel's name from the shelves of your school library, as he is now also a very successful children's author.

The song that Baddiel, Skinner and Broudie wrote was called 'Three Lions'. It was sung in homes and pubs and stadiums around the country, and it still is. Alongside 'Nessun Dorma' it quickly became an anthem for football fans. Especially English ones.

And it still is.

EURO 96

1996

Euro 96 was not going to plan. Football might not be coming home after all.

England's first game found them 1–0 up at half-time, but they conceded a late goal from opponents Switzerland. A 1–1 draw: a disappointment. But there were still matches against Scotland and the Netherlands to come.

England v their 'auld enemy', Scotland. The oldest international football game in the world. And it began well – with the last ten minutes in sight, England were 1–0 up. Could they avoid conceding a late equaliser this time?

Maybe not. Because... after a Tony Adams tackle went wrong, Scotland were awarded a penalty.

The crowd swallowed. Not again. And not against Scotland.

But then, Leeds United and Scotland midfielder, Gary McAllister, missed his penalty. And a minute later, one of the greatest goals in England history was scored.

The England keeper David Seaman cleared the ball. A long punt up field. He knew there were players up there who could damage the deflated Scots.

Teddy Sheringham controlled the ball, knocked it to Darren Anderton, who, seeing Paul Gascoigne running on goal, passed it through to him.

People were on their feet as Gazza let the ball bounce towards goal, then lofted it over Colin Hendry, beating the defender to blast the ball past Goram.

If you listen to the crowd there was a roar of anticipation when Gazza beat Hendry.

Then, a moment of silence, as if the whole Wembley crowd was holding its breath, the ball seeming to hang in the air before it connected with Gazza's boot.

Then, a roar when the net billowed and Gazza ran to celebrate.

Literally, a breathtaking goal.

PERFECT DAY

1996

When England met the Netherlands in their final group game of Euro 96, something felt different.

Wembley Stadium was bathed in sunshine. It was a perfect day.

England looked irresistible. Was something going to happen? Were the 30 years of hurt about to end?

England were not renowned for beating the other big teams of Europe by big margins. But after edging past Scotland, by 2–0 in their previous game, confidence was up.

And England certainly had a dynamic duo up front. Alan Shearer and Teddy Sheringham were both strikers at the top of their game. And both scored twice in a game that shocked the orange shirt-wearing Dutch team. England 4, The Netherlands 1.

The atmosphere in the stadium was electric. As it

was in homes and pubs in villages, towns and cities across the country. It really did feel like football was coming home. That England were going to win the tournament.

If they were, though, England would have to beat Spain in their quarter-final.

FAILURE IS NOT TAKING A PENALTY

1996

In justifying why he wanted to take the third penalty in the Euro 96 quarter-final against Spain, Stuart Pearce made it clear what a footballer should do in a game's most crucial moments.

'Failure is not taking a penalty,' he said.

This from the man who – along with Chris Waddle – had missed a penalty in the 1990 World Cup semi-final against West Germany, when England got so close.

'Not if I stepped up and missed again,' Pearce went on to say. 'That's not failure.'

What Pearce said – and what he did that day at Wembley – sums up what sport is all about, and what life is all about.

Step up.

If you miss, you miss. But always step up.

Stuart Pearce stepped up. He blasted the ball past the Spanish keeper. Then – after hesitating for a half-second – he punched the air once, twice, three times, his face contorted with emotion.

England beat Spain on penalties. Now they faced Germany in the semi-final. A game that would also end in a penalty shoot-out.

THE MAKING OF GARETH SOUTHGATE

1996

Sir Gareth Southgate is acknowledged as the second most successful England manager of all time – second only to Sir Alf Ramsey – since his retirement after the 2024 Euros.

Over eight years from 2016, Southgate managed the team in four major tournaments, in which they reached two finals, a semi-final and a quarter-final.

It now feels normal that England should feature in the last four or even last two of a tournament. But this didn't used to be the case – not until Sir Gareth took over.

Arguably, the roots of Southgate's exceptional stint as England manager date back to the Euros 1996 semi-final against Germany, when he was still a player.

After a 1–1 draw, and ten converted penalties, it was Southgate's turn to take a spot-kick. If he missed, England would once again lose on penalties to Germany in a tournament semi-final.

Southgate stepped up. Put it to the keeper's right. But it was not wide enough and the keeper, diving the right way, saved it easily.

Southgate looked broken.

Just as Stuart Pearce had suffered in 1990, a brutal chant followed Southgate around the stadiums of England in the later days of his career:

Who let his country down?

Gareth Southgate.

Gareth Southgate.

Sir Gareth has since spoken about a letter he received after his 1996 miss, which said that there was nothing to be done about our past and that we could only influence our future.

That letter helped him in a decisive way. He would use his past miss to create a positive future.

What a future that would be.

DER BALL

1996

When a player scores a hat-trick, traditionally they get to keep the match ball. As a souvenir of their achievement. Even in a World Cup Final.

But at the end of the 1966 Final, while the England players celebrated becoming world champions, it was the scorer of the game's first goal – Helmut Haller – who stuffed the ball up his white West Germany top.

Haller was an opportunist, both with his early goal in the game as well as his hiding of the ball post-match.

For three decades the ball's whereabouts remained a mystery.

And then in 1996, on the 30th anniversary of the win, Haller reappeared to return the ball back to England, explaining that he had kept the ball all that time in his cellar.

Now Der Ball sits as a prize exhibit at the English National Museum of Football.

A GLORIOUS GOALLESS DRAW

1997

To qualify for the next World Cup finals, France 1998, England would have to do it the hard way. They were drawn in the same group as Italy, then three-times winners of the tournament. Only one team, the host nation of France, and the holders of the trophy (Brazil on this occasion) could qualify automatically.

It seemed clear that Italy would now qualify automatically for the World Cup. At England's expense. Unless England could win in Rome when they met a second time at qualifying stage.

But, while Italy stumbled to goalless draws in Poland and Georgia, England went on to flourish. They went on to do the double on all the other teams in their group.

In England's penultimate group game, against Moldova, they won 4–0 with two goals from Arsenal's

Ian Wright, playing in only his ninth game for his country after working his way through non-league football to become a professional footballer.

Because Italy had dropped four points, they now had one point fewer than England.

One game left. In Rome. Italy v England.

England didn't need to win. Only to draw.

Glenn Hoddle managed the game perfectly on the touchline and Paul Ince led the team on to the pitch. Ince took a cut to the head in the 12th minute and played most of the game with a bandaged head, needing stitches midway through the second half. Channelling his inner Terry Butcher, Ince did what he needed to. And England held out against Baggio, Vieri and Del Piero to secure the 0–0 draw they needed. England were going to France 1998.

At the final whistle, Ian Wright ripped his shirt off, and shouted, over and over, 'I'm going to the World Cup!'

ENGLAND WIN A TOURNAMENT

1997

In 1997 the French hosted a small-scale international tournament called Tournoi de France.

There was a year to go until France would host their second World Cup finals. They wanted 1998 to be perfect, and this would be a great way for them to prepare both on the pitch and off it.

They invited Brazil, England and Italy to join them – three of the six countries to have won the World Cup up to that point.

Each team would play each other once. In a league format, like a World Cup group set-up.

All the games not involving England ended in draws. So, even though England lost to 1–0 to Brazil in their final game, England finished top because they had beaten Italy 2–0 and France 1–0.

This was the final table:

Pos	Team	Pld	W	D	L	F-A	Pts
1	**England**	3	2	0	1	3–1	6
2	**Brazil**	3	1	2	0	5–4	5
3	**France**	3	0	2	1	3–4	2
4	**Italy**	3	0	2	1	5–7	2

England had won a tournament!

Could they carry that kind of form into the 1998 World Cup finals?

KEY TO TABLES:

Pos – position

Pld – games played;

W – games won;

D – games drawn;

L – games lost;

F – for (goals scored);

A – against (goals conceded);

Pts – total points earned by the team in the league

FRANCE 1998

1998

England qualified relatively easily from Group G at the France '98 World Cup finals group, beating Tunisia 2–0 and Colombia 2–0, although losing to Romania 2–1, who went on to top the group.

Two wins was sufficient for England to also reach the knockout stages, but now they faced a Round of 16 tie against old rivals Argentina.

In World Cup knockout history, England had beaten Argentina in 1966, but had lost in 1986.

Who would come out on top this time?

It was an eventful game. At half-time, it was 2–2, and the second half was only just underway when David Beckham was shoulder-barged and wound up sprawling on the ground. A clear foul. But then, the Manchester United midfielder lifted his boot to kick at Diego Simeone.

Right in front of the referee.

Beckham was sent off!

England were down to ten men for the whole of the second half, and for extra time. Would they have won with David Beckham on the pitch? Probably. He was the best player in the world. Or certainly one of them.

The game ended 2–2. And England lost on penalties, with David Batty and Paul Ince missing theirs.

But it was Beckham, not the penalty-missers, who faced all the rage of the fans back home. Still a young man at 23, he became possibly the most hated man in Britain for a time, with abuse from the media and from the terraces. It was brutal.

But look at David Beckham now – a national treasure, who was knighted in 2025. Sir David.

Perhaps the game against Argentina should instead be remembered for Michael Owen's goal that put England 2–1 up after only 16 minutes. Only 18 years old at the beginning of his England career, Owen took control of the ball in the centre circle, and then with exceptional pace, ran through two tackles, drew the keeper and fired the ball into the net.

It was one of the great World Cup goals. A goal that deserved to win a game. But it didn't.

SCHOLES SKINS SCOTS

1999

England came second to Sweden in their qualifying group for Euro 2000. Consequently, for them to reach the finals in Belgium and the Netherlands, they would have to compete in a play-off consisting of two games. One home. One away.

Who would they draw? Slovenia? Ukraine? Israel?

No. It was Scotland.

In the early days of World Cup qualification, England and Scotland had faced play-offs to reach the finals in 1950 and 1954. England had won through both times. Would the result for Euro 2000 be the same? Or would Scotland embarrass their 'auld enemy'?

The second game at Wembley ended England 0 Scotland 1. Fortunately, for England, the first game – at Scotland's Hampden Park – ended Scotland 0 England 2.

Both goals that got England to the finals in Belgium and the Netherlands were scored by Paul Scholes, one of the most underrated footballers of recent times.

Scholes was a superb midfielder, but he was often overshadowed by other players who he supplied with passes and tackled back for at Manchester United, players like David Beckham, Roy Keane, Eric Cantona and Wayne Rooney.

Scholes was a player's player. No fuss. He just did it.

And he most definitely did it against Scotland.

He scored his first goal with a deft shot that exposed gaps in the Scottish defence. His second came from a header from a David Beckham free kick. One of the shorter players on the pitch, Scholes punished the Scots for lax defending.

WEMBLEY

2000

England's last game at the old Wembley before a major rebuild of the stadium was a World Cup qualifier in October 2000, against England's great rival. Germany.

Who better to play a Wembley finale against than the team England had beaten in the 1966 World Cup final.

It was a difficult game. An organised – but dull – German side contained England who seemed to lack the tactical intelligence to break down the defence.

England lost. Qualification for Japan/Korea in 2002 was looking in jeopardy. England would have to win well in the second leg of the game in Germany. An unlikely scenario.

The real drama of the night came half an hour after the end of the game. The England coach, Kevin Keegan, one of the greatest England footballers ever,

and twice winner of the Ballon d'Or, came out to face
the TV cameras.

Known for his straight talking, the Yorkshireman
told the world that he had just resigned as England
manager.

Kevin Keegan was not good enough as England
manager. He knew it. But, unlike many of those
who came before and after him, he was at least good
enough to admit it.

5-1

2001

Germany had never lost a home World Cup qualifier. Ever.

Meanwhile, England – having lost to Germany 1–0 at Wembley in the home game – needed a win away against them to have a hope of getting to the 2002 World Cup in South Korea and Japan.

Since the 1966 World Cup final the two teams had played 16 times, but England winning three, drawing two, and losing 11 if you include penalty shoot-outs.

And those 11 losses included three devastating defeats (1970, 1990, 1996) that each put England out of tournaments.

The omens were not good. The history was not good.

But Michael Owen was good. He was fast. Fast and young and dangerous. England had David Beckham and Steven Gerrard and Emile Heskey, too, all players who already had stellar careers in football.

Could England, under their new Swedish manager, Sven-Göran Eriksson, do something?

It started unpromisingly when Germany took a 1–0 lead in the sixth minute.

Then.

England.

Tore.

Germany.

Apart.

A powerful half-volley from 25 yards from Gerrard. A beautiful run on goal and shot from Heskey. But it was Michael Owen who did the real damage: three goals.

Owen's last goal was scored on 66 minutes. Sixty-six: a good number for England.

ENGLAND ON TOUR

2000

From 2001 until 2007, England played their home games away from Wembley. With a new national stadium being built, they had no choice. But it wasn't a bad thing; it was a good thing.

Before 2000, there was a feeling round the country that it was unfair for the national team to play all its games in the far south-east of the country, hundreds of miles away from, and beyond the budget of, most ordinary football fans. Wayne Rooney was from Liverpool, and Nigel Martyn hailed from Cornwall… so why did the games always have to be in London?

Now they didn't have to be.

During those out-of-Wembley years, England toured 14 different stadiums, from Leeds to Leicester and from Sunderland to Southampton in those out-of-Wembley years.

Since then, the England team has had a stronger appeal because of the bond it created with all their fans, instead of only the ones in the south-east or only those who could afford to travel to and stay in the south-east.

Although now that all the England games seem to be played at Wembley once again… maybe the FA needs to remember where all of its fans and players come from.

THE ONE WITH THE BECKHAM FREE KICK

2002

It was the last round of games in UEFA Group 9. England v Greece. Germany v Finland.

All England had to do was get a better result than the Germans and they were through to the 2002 Korea/Japan World Cup finals.

But football rarely stays on script. There are always twists and turns, and sometimes there are last-minute free kicks.

With 68 minutes gone, England were 1–0 down against Greece. Over in Germany it was still 0–0. Then Teddy Sheringham got onto the end of a Beckham free kick and looped the ball into the net.

It was 1–1! England fans celebrated. England were now topping their group. But only for one minute. Because in the 69th minute, Greece scored again.

They were celebrating in Germany now.

At the very end, England had another free kick: 30–35 yards out. David Beckham stepped up and eyed the crowd. This was Old Trafford. His stadium. His England team, as captain.

News was about to come through that Germany had drawn 0–0 with Finland. England needed Beckham to score this goal, to secure a 2–2 draw and qualification for Korea/Japan.

Could Beckham, the icon of the England game, do it? Could he wipe away the misery of that petulant exit from the 1998 World Cup with one strike of the ball?

Beckham composed himself. He moved towards the ball. He hit it.

The Greek keeper didn't move.

The ball hit the back of the net.

Job done.

England were going to the 2002 World Cup.

2002

For the World Cup finals in South Korea and Japan, England were drawn in a hard group. It was nicknamed 'the group of death', a name normally given to the toughest group to be drawn in.

England were up against Sweden, a challenging European side; Nigeria, a strong African team; and Argentina. Again.

Although England had beaten Argentina on their way to winning the trophy in 1966, they then lost both times when they met in competitive games: Mexico 86 and France 98.

It couldn't go on like that.

Fortunately, it didn't.

England took the lead late in the first half with a David Beckham penalty. The second half saw the South Americans attack in wave after wave from

Gabriel Batistuta, Verón, Hernán Crespo and Diego Simeone. But the England defence – Leeds United pair Danny Mills and Rio Ferdinand, and Arsenal pair Sol Campbell and Ashley Cole – stood firm.

England held on with a solid defensive display to beat the Argentinians 1–0, which all but secured them qualification for the knockout stages.

They easily beat Denmark 3–0 in the Round of 16 but then they lost 2–1 to the eventual champions, Brazil. The Brazil team boasting the likes of Ronaldo, Rivaldo, Ronaldinho and Roberto Carlos.

Not a bad World Cup for England, though. Beat your two biggest rivals on the way, then lose only to the eventual winners.

2003

On 12 February 2003, a 17-year-old came on as a substitute in an England friendly game against Australia at West Ham's Upton Park Stadium.

He was the youngest player to be selected for England. The youngest since the Clapham Rovers player James Prinsep played in 1879.

One hundred and twenty-four years later, Wayne Rooney of Everton superseded him. He was 17 and 111 days old.

While Prinsep played only that one game for England, Rooney went on to be one of the greatest England players. He was the most gifted player of his generation.

Rooney played 120 times for England's men's team. This after previously representing the U15, U17 and U19 teams.

He scored 53 goals. And went to three World Cups and three European Championships finals.

Only in 2008 was Rooney superseded as the youngest player ever to start for England – by Arsenal's Theo Walcott.

2004

Euro 2004 took place in Portugal, and England qualified for their place in style. Top of their group with six wins and two draws. No defeats.

And why wouldn't they have qualified – given that their squad included players like Owen, Lampard, Beckham and Cole. What was known as the Golden Generation.

England were drawn in another 'group of death', in competition with France, Croatia and Switzerland. They came second by beating the Swiss, beating the Croats and only losing to France 2–1.

England went into the quarter-finals full of a hope of glory. Even in their game against the hosts, Portugal, there really was hope. A hope of glory. Especially after England took the lead after three minutes through Michael Owen.

But the game fluctuated. Portugal equalised late. Extra time was needed. Portugal took the lead in extra time. Then England equalised.

Yo-yo football again.

Penalties again.

And – you guessed it – defeat again.

Germany 2006

England were a definite contender to win at the 2006 World Cup finals. They had their Golden Generation, after all. Lampard. Rooney. Beckham. Gerrard. And the rest.

All this, and they were managed by a man considered to be one of the great football managers working at the time. The Swede, Sven-Göran Eriksson.

Hopes were high. The recipe for success looked tasty.

And the tournament began well for England. Topping their group with wins against Paraguay, and then Trinidad and Tobago, plus a draw with Sweden, before winning against Ecuador in the Round of 16.

Now England faced a depleted Portugal in the quarter-finals.

England looked the better team. On paper, they

should have won. On the grass of the Gelsenkirchen pitch, they should have won. If only the thing that happened had not happened.

But it happened. After being manhandled by two Portuguese players trying to get the ball off him, Rooney trod on Ricardo Carvalho as he lay on the ground. And he was sent off.

Rooney's teammate at Manchester United – Cristiano Ronaldo – winked at the Portugal bench when this happened, deflecting the anger and disappointment of the England fans from Rooney to the Portuguese legend. England fans were furious with Ronaldo, not Rooney.

The game ended 0–0 and in the ensuing shoot-out, England missed three of their four penalties, losing 3–1.

Would England have won if Rooney had not been sent off? They missed his contribution for a whole hour of normal and extra time.

WEMBLEY 2.0

2007

When England reopened the new Wembley Stadium to their fans, Brazil were invited to join them. Seven years in the making, Wembley 2.0 was an impressive venue.

It was built to hold 90,000 fans. It cost £798 million to build. Outside, you could find a statue of Bobby Moore.

It was fitting that the FA invited Brazil to be England's first opponents. As we saw earlier, Brazil had done the same for England in 1984, and it was important to show gratitude for that, and also to show respect to the greatest team in the history of football.

Some real legends were present on the pitch for the special game. Ronaldinho, Kaká and Robinho played for Brazil against Beckham, Lampard, Owen and Gerrard for England.

It was John Terry who looked to have won it for England, with a well-placed header from a Beckham free kick on 68 minutes.

But as ever, Brazil never gave up. That is one reason why they have won the most World Cups.

Two minutes into injury time, Diego netted.

And the game ended 1–1.

But a new Wembley era had begun. With Steve McClaren as England's new manager – though not for long.

2010

Under Steve McClaren, England had failed to qualify for the 2008 Euros. McClaren's replacement was their second foreign manager – and this time it was an Italian: Fabio Capello. He helped them in their efforts to qualify for the 2010 World Cup in South Africa.

England got through the group stages, but with a 1–0 win over Slovenia and draws with the USA and Algeria, they finished second in their group. Their performance had been uninspiring. They felt more like a collection of players than a team that gelled.

And their weak showing at group stage did not bode well for their Round of 16 knockout game against Germany.

Tough. Very tough.

And it seemed to begin that way. England were outplayed and found themselves 2–0 down. Then, against the run of play, Matthew Upson headed a goal back.

There was hope. A lot of hope. Especially with what happened next on the pitch that day.

At 2–1, England had improved and when Frank Lampard's thunderstrike hit the bar and bounced over the line, they appeared to have equalised. Clearly.

England celebrated. But the goal was not given. The referee and linesmen did not see it cross the line, even though tens of millions had on the TV replay. Capello was fuming. Beckham was outraged.

It was referred to by the Germans as a 'ghost goal', triggering memories of England's goal in the 1966 World Cup final.

The disallowed Lampard goal played a huge role in changing football history and the creation of VAR.

England had been robbed. They went on to lose 4–1.

If you watch the highlights of the game, you can see that Germany were the better side.

Still – it wasn't fair.

2012

England had a good group stage in the 2012 European Championships, jointly held in Poland and Ukraine. Even though it was far from easy.

France. Always difficult. But England managed a 1–1 draw.

Ukraine. One of the host countries, of course. England won 1–0.

Sweden. A good solid European team. England won 3–2.

Top of their group, England qualified for the quarter-finals, and their manager, Roy Hodgson, was confident. Only Germany and Spain had a better track record at group stage. Surely England could hope for a place in the semi-final, maybe even the final.

England had to beat Italy in the quarter-finals. Italy were a good team – perhaps not a great team –

although they usually did well at tournament football.

The game ended 0–0. While Italy dominated possession, number of passes completed and shots on target, England played a stubborn, defensive game.

And then it came to penalties.

Gerrard scored. Rooney scored. Then England missed their next two and they were on the plane home.

Defeated on penalties. Again.

2014

England reached the finals of the 2014 World Cup, hosted by Brazil. They did so by qualifying undefeated: six wins and four draws. They finished above Ukraine and Poland, their main rivals.

To qualify was good. But for England, Brazil 2014 just went downhill from there:

A defeat to Italy, who – along with England – would fail to pass the group stages. A defeat to Uruguay, who would lose to Colombia in the Round of 16. And a draw with Costa Rica. It was dismal.

Roy Hodgson stayed on as England manager, but Steven Gerrard retired from international football as soon as the tournament was over. Frank Lampard did the same a few weeks later.

The Golden Generation was done.

Another disappointing World Cup for England.

2016

For England, Euro 2016 in France brought – as all tournaments will do – its highs and its lows.

The high was the group game against Wales.

This was a good Wales team – Gareth Bale at its heart, scaring the defenders of Europe – and they defeated Slovakia and Russia at group stage. Later they would beat Northern Ireland, and even a very strong Belgium – with Kevin De Bruyne, Eden Hazard and Romelu Lukaku all in the team.

But could Wales beat England, too?

To lose to Wales would not be good. England fans would never hear the last of it. Just like Wales rugby fans never hear the last of when England have won the rugby union World Cup and they have not.

Predictably, Bale put Wales ahead on 42 minutes. But England equalised through Jamie Vardy on 56.

And then Daniel Sturridge scored the winner in injury time.

England 2 Wales 1.

A sweet day.

But unlike Wales, England failed to beat Slovakia and Russia in their group, so they only came second. And in the knockout stage, they faced Iceland. Which is when things froze up.

No one thought England (population: 55 million) would lose to Iceland (population: 335,000).

But they did.

SOUTHGATE

2016

After England's defeat to Iceland at Euro 2016, manager Roy Hodgson resigned as manager.

England then appointed Sam Allardyce. He lasted just 67 days, then was sacked for inappropriate conduct. Something to do with money.

What would the team do now? It was a mess. Beaten by Iceland. Managerial disappointment. A golden generation losing its shine.

With the senior team doing so poorly, there was some hope on the horizon. At least the U21s were doing well. They had lost only five of their 39 matches over three years, and they had some amazing young players coming through.

Their manager was Gareth Southgate.

And it was to Southgate that England turned. He was promoted from the U21s to the senior team.

As you will see in the rest of this book, Southgate's focus on teamwork, valuing his players, honesty with each other and on doing the right thing, all created a culture in the England camp that led to the most successful time for the England men's team…

… since 1966 and all that.

BANANA SKIN

2017

As England manager, Gareth Southgate knew about pressure as a footballer. During his playing career, he had played a total of over 500 games for Crystal Palace, Aston Villa and Middlesbrough.

Also, 57 games for England. Including that infamous penalty miss in 1996.

His senior managerial career with England began when they faced a not-too-tough World Cup qualifying group against Slovakia, Slovenia, Malta, Lithuania and Scotland. The target: Russia 2018.

The biggest threat of all of those was Scotland – that was a potential banana skin. But England were sailing through the group. Four wins, including a 3–0 at home to Scotland. Looking good. Until they faced Scotland for a second time. At Hampden Park.

This was the banana skin. Scotland away is always

a challenge. Especially for England. Hampden Park is the stadium where England have lost the most games.

A tense game seemed won when England took the lead with a 70th-minute goal from Alex Oxlade-Chamberlain.

But within the last five minutes of normal play, Scotland were awarded two free kicks from 25 yards out. Two Lee Griffiths free kicks.

And Griffiths scored both: in the 87th minute and then the 90th.

Scotland thought they had won. The 90 minutes was up now.

Deep into injury time, England were attacking frenetically. This wasn't just about qualifying for Russia. It was about pride. England didn't want to lose to Scotland. It was worse than losing to Wales.

A deep cross for England. Gaps opening in the Scottish penalty area. Tired legs. Players out of position. An air of panic was now rippling around the Scotland stadium.

But there was Harry Kane. Doing what he does so well. In the right place at the right time.

At 2–2, thanks to Kane's last-minute goal, England had held their nerve against Scotland. They went on to win their next four games and ended the group qualifiers with eight wins and two draws.

These were solid foundations for Southgate's first qualifying campaign on the pitch. But off the pitch, things were solid too. There was a clear change of culture. The young players that Southgate had brought through from the U21s wanted to play for their manager. And for each other.

There was hope. Hope for Russia 2018. Hope for Gareth Southgate's first finals.

2018

England had played three penalty shoot-outs in World Cup finals. Germany at Italia 90. Argentina at France 1998. Portugal at Germany 2006.

They had lost them all.

England failed when it came to penalties. The world knew this. It was a thing.

At 2018's Russia World Cup finals, England finished second in their group, after beating Tunisia and Panama and losing to Belgium. Next they faced Colombia in the Round of 16.

This was knockout football. Win and you're through. Draw and it's penalties.

The Colombia game ended 1–1. Harry Kane had scored again to find himself as leading tournament scorer: six goals in four games.

But it was still a draw. And so, again, to penalties.

Kane scored. Rashford scored. But when Jordan Henderson missed, England found themselves 3–2 down.

It looked bleak.

But this was Gareth Southgate's team.

Trippier scored. Dier scored. And Colombia missed their last two.

It was hard to believe… but England had actually won a penalty shoot-out in the World Cup finals. Something had changed.

Southgate's team went on to win their quarter-final against Sweden but lost to Croatia in their semi-final.

But England had still reached the World Cup semi-final for only the third time in their history. Furthermore, they had won a penalty shoot-out for the first time. And their striker, Harry Kane, was the tournament's leading scorer.

This was success. Could they push on, and maybe reach a tournament final? Maybe even win one?

It was beginning to feel a bit like they could. One day…

EURO 2020

2021

Euro 2020 was unusual for three reasons.

One. It was hosted by multiple nations. Not just one country.

Two. It was played in stadiums that were not full. The world was only just emerging from the worst of the Covid pandemic, so the tournament had been delayed by a year, and crowds were limited.

And three. England reached the final.

They had achieved this via wins against Croatia and the Czech Republic in the group stages. (And a 0–0 draw with Scotland.) Then they knocked out Germany, Ukraine and Denmark.

It bears repeating: England were in the final. Their first final since 1966.

And in Raheem Sterling they had a goal machine at their disposal. Sterling had scored the winning goals against Croatia, the Czechs and the Germans. He was on fire.

Ten team goals scored and only one conceded. Five wins out of six. These were crazy days.

But stop… let's rewind for a moment… to the Round of 16.

England 2 Germany 0?

Was this for real? The last time England had beaten Germany in a knockout game was 55 years earlier. And on that occasion, 1966, they had won the tournament.

Now England fans were asking the question… Could it happen again? Would England win a major championship final? At Wembley?

With this in mind, they prepared to play Italy in the final.

FINAL

2021

Euro 2020, staged a year late due to the pandemic, saw Italy and England play each other in the final under the floodlights at Wembley Stadium in London.

England lost. On penalties.

For England fans it was a sad night, but was it a failure?

In one way, yes. Every team that took part – from France to Germany to Spain – that failed to reach the final also failed to win.

But in another way, this was success. England had led 1–0 for over an hour. Luke Shaw had scored the fastest ever goal in a European Championship final. In under two minutes.

Compare that with the many tournaments in the 1970s, 1980s and 1990s that England did not reach.

To lose in a final is sad, but it is still a success. Of a kind. It is better that losing in a semi-final or a quarter-final.

Or of not even being there.

KALVIN PHILLIPS

2021

When Bukayo Saka missed his penalty in the Euro 2020 final shoot-out against Italy, the dream was over.

Italy had won.

There is a lot of footage of that moment, captured by a range of devices, from TV cameras to mobile phones.

One extraordinary angle of the game came from a drone high above Wembley.

It showed a tiny figure in white step up to take the penalty. A tiny figure in yellow stopped the ball. Then a dozen or more tiny figures in blue ran past the tiny figure in white to mob the one in yellow.

The Italy team were celebrating with their keeper. They were the European champions.

The figure in white stood alone.

Briefly.

Then another tiny figure in white moved quickly towards him.

It was his teammate. He was there to console Saka, to praise him for stepping up in the first place.

Kalvin Phillips was that teammate.

Later that year, Kalvin Phillips received the England Player of the Year award for 2020–21.

2022

By 2022, under Gareth Southgate, England were used to reaching finals and semi-finals in major tournaments, so a quarter-final exit at Qatar 2022 almost felt like a failure.

But admittedly, England lost in those quarter-finals to France. Yes, Mbappé's France. The France who reached the final, scored three goals and lost only on penalties, to Argentina's Messi and his teammates.

Things had been going so well for England until the France game. It had been a successful tournament.

Up to and including the Round of 16, no team had scored more goals than England. They'd managed 12 in just four games with a 6–2 win over Iran, 3–0 wins over both Wales and Senegal, and a 0–0 draw with the USA. Of England's tally of 12 goals, Saka and Rashford each contributed three.

And in the quarter-final against France, England had the stats on their side:

Possession   54% to 46%

Shots   14–9

Shots on target   6–5

But the stats that matter are goals scored. And France won that battle 2–1, with the winner coming from Olivier Giroud.

It was not a bad World Cup for England – at least they weren't knocked out of a tournament by Iceland this time. At least it was a very good French team.

HARRY KANE

When Harry Kane scored his 54th goal for England, he broke the much-coveted record eyed by every English goal scorer.

For Harry Kane was now England's leading goal scorer.

His record-breaker came during a Euro 2024 qualifier against Italy. The first game in Group C. You couldn't expect a more difficult opening game than Italy away. And not in any old Italian city, but in Naples in front of a tough local crowd.

At the start of the match, England's top five goal scorers in history were:

Rooney 53

Kane 53

Charlton B 49

Lineker 48

Greaves 44

When Kane scored with his penalty, he moved ahead
of Wayne Rooney in the all-time rankings. He had
scored more goals than any England male footballer
ever. An astonishing feat.

For the record books, Harry Kane scored 52 of
his first 54 inside the penalty area, the remaining
two outside. Six with his left foot, nine with his head
and 39 with his right foot.

Hats off to Harry! As for England, they were off
to a good start in qualifying for Germany 2024. And
with Harry Kane only 29, the question was how many
would he score for his country before he retired. (And
at the time of writing, at the end of 2025, Kane has
now scored 78 goals! At that rate, how much further
can he still go? Can he reach 100?)

2024

Euro 2024 in Germany had been okay for England. Well… okayish.

In their group games they beat Serbia 1–0, and then drew with Denmark and Slovenia. And to be fair, England did top their group. You couldn't do better than that, could you?

But there was a feeling that the team was playing way below people's expectations. Two goals in three games. No player really shining – not yet anyway. So much had been expected of England's young players, especially Jude Bellingham, who had just turned 21 that weekend.

In the Round of 16 knockout game against Slovakia, England were 1–0 down, five minutes into second-half injury time.

Down and out, or so it seemed, England seemed

to be in a desperate position. Loading the Slovakia penalty area with players, they had one last chance.

A long throw reached Crystal Palace's Marc Guéhi. The ball skimmed into a crowd of players – and there was Jude Bellingham. Back to goal. But in the air. An overhead kick. The ball in the back of the net.

The England players ran in a stream of white shirts to celebrate with Bellingham. They were still in it. An equaliser at the death. An amazing strike.

England 1 Slovakia 1.

Thanks to Bellingham, the game had gone into extra time. One minute in, Harry Kane scored the winner and England were heading into the quarter-finals.

2024

England played five tight games before they reached the semi-final of Euro 2024. Every game was close. Every game was low scoring. No three-nils or six-twos this time.

In the Round of 16, as we've seen, they beat Slovakia after extra time, thanks to that late Jude Bellingham strike. Then, in the quarter-finals, they beat Switzerland after extra time and on penalties.

Next up – in the semi-final – it was the Netherlands. A team including Cody Gakpo, Virgil van Dijk and Memphis Depay.

England's presence in the semi-finals might have felt low key and they might not have destroyed all their opponents. But this was only the third time England had reached the Euro semi-finals. And that was good. Very good.

After 90 minutes, it was 1–1. An early goal by the Dutch had been cancelled out by a Harry Kane penalty.

Would England need extra time again? Like they had in the round of 16 and the quarter-finals?

The answer was no. They scored their winner late. Very late.

But it was a beautiful goal. A team goal. Direct and skilful.

Declan Rice passed the ball from the centre circle. Cole Palmer received it, controlled it and knocked it forward, having looked up to see Aston Villa's Ollie Watkins racing towards the penalty area. Two quick passes along the ground. Rice, then Palmer. The England players moving around each other like a machine.

Now Watkins has it, back to goal. Three Dutch defenders have been taken out by Palmer's pass. Watkins, one defender and the keeper to beat, turns and hits a shot so hard the defender can't block it, and the keeper can't even see it as it flashes across him and into the inside of the side netting.

It was 2–1 to England. No time for the Dutch to reply.

England had reached their second Euro final in a row.

Unfortunately, they would also lose their second final in a row, too. Spain this time.

But reaching a final is still a success. And quite possibly, next time… in the next tournament… maybe England will go one stage further.

PERFECT

2025

Thomas Tuchel was the first German to manage England, and the team's qualifying campaign for the 2026 World Cup was perfect.

Played eight. Won eight.

Scored 22.

Conceded none.

Goals from 11 different players, with Harry Kane (8) and Eberechi Eze (3) leading the way.

This was a team. Teams win games. Teams qualify for tournaments. Teams end up topping their groups.

But it takes a real team, coached well, with a togetherness, to go through all eight qualifiers without conceding a goal.

What does this mean for England's hopes in the World Cup finals 2026?

We shall see…

England have drawn Croatia, Ghana and Panama in the World Cup this time. Not an easy group for them, but also not too difficult.

But that page has yet to be written.

2026

This World Cup is about you. Don't forget that.

You might think it is about Jude Bellingham, Jack Grealish, Harry Kane or Thomas Tuchel. But it is really about you.

You will remember this tournament for the rest of your life. The goals. The games. The victories. Or maybe, the defeat that ended it all and made you feel sad.

You'll remember other teams' games. The unexpected team that beats one of the world's elite.

And other teams' players, too. The way a player celebrates a last-minute goal.

You will remember where you watched the games, and who you were with. You will remember things you eat and drink, and what happened the next day at school.

World Cups are weird like that. They are great.

And, when you watch World Cups in 2030 and 2034 and beyond, you will remember 2026 and smile, even if things didn't go England's way.

This book is for you. I hope your experience of the 2026 World Cup is like the one I had in 1990.

But better.

Read on for a sneak preview of
another brilliant football story by
Tom Palmer. . .

Liverpool's Greatest Moments

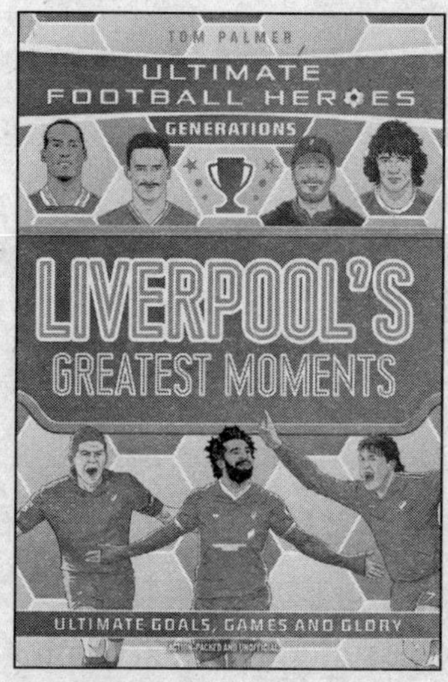

Available now!

CHAMPIONS OF ENGLAND. AGAIN.

English Champions # 20

On 25 April 2025 Liverpool lined up against Tottenham Hotspur at Anfield, needing a draw to be named English champions.

In front of their loyal fans. At their home stadium, Anfield.

And to do it for a record-equalling 20th time.

Although Liverpool had won the league just five years before in 2020, that season had been troubled by the Covid-19 pandemic and the fans could not enjoy that glorious moment of becoming champions in person.

In 2025 it would be different.

Anfield was full and more than 60,000 fans were there to witness it, with millions cheering them on around the world.

All fans, regardless of team, were moved by the

singing of 'You'll Never Walk Alone' as they watched the Liverpool players form a huddle on the pitch.

The game?

It ended 5–1. More proof that Liverpool were undeniably the best men's football club in England. Liverpool were champions.

At the end of the season, even though they failed to win any of their last four games, their record was astonishing. A lead of ten points over their nearest rivals, Arsenal. 25 wins out of 38 games. 84 points and 86 goals scored. Clearly the best team in England. By a long way.

Liverpool had dominated the top flight of the English league throughout the 2024–25 season and had secured their 20th league title, tying at 20–20 with Manchester United. Liverpool's six Champions League wins against Manchester's three meant that Liverpool were now the greatest team in the history of the England game.

You can read about their other 19 league titles and the other thirty or so trophies in the rest of this book, alongside some other marvellous moments in the history of our greatest football team.

ENGLISH PREMIER LEAGUE								
	P	W	D	L	F	A	GD	Pts
Liverpool	38	25	9	4	86	41	+45	84
Arsenal	38	20	14	4	69	34	+35	74
Man City	38	21	8	9	72	44	+28	71

TOP OF THE LEAGUE

English Champions # 20

In winning their 20th league title, Liverpool finally caught up with Manchester United to become one of two teams to have jointly won the most English league titles.

Liverpool had been top of this league of leagues until 2009 when Manchester United joined them on 18 titles, taking over Liverpool as outright leaders with 19 titles in 2011.

Manchester United's supremacy over Liverpool lasted 14 years.

For the record, the top five English title-winning teams of all time are:

Liverpool	20
Man United	20
Arsenal	13
Man City	10
Everton	9

The 2025–26 season might see Liverpool or Manchester United take a lead with 21 titles.

Based on their performance in 2024–25 it seems likely that the first team to reach 21 will be Liverpool.

But that is all in the future…

Liverpool Women F.C.

Liverpool women finished the 2024–2025 Women's Super League in seventh position. That is out of 12 teams in the WSL. A solid season with the team established as a top flight team in a season with an exciting end.

The exciting end?

The Lionesses attempting to regain the EUROs during the summer.

Liverpool Women F.C. – as you might know – were instrumental in helping to create a women's league that can deliver a tournament-winning England team. What Liverpool did to help create a professional game in England was a game changer. You will read more about how that all came about later in the book.

Liverpool reached the semi-finals of the FA Cup in 2024–25, losing to the best team in England, Chelsea.

It was a good season, if not a great season. And one thing Liverpool can take from it is finishing above their local rivals, Everton.

The future is bright for Liverpool F.C. and the Lionesses.

SALAH AND VAN DIJK SIGN CONTRACT EXTENSIONS

Players

There was a point in spring 2025 when it looked like Liverpool were going to lose three of their very best players on free transfers.

The contracts of Trent Alexander-Arnold, Mo Salah and Virgil van Dijk were all coming to an end as the 2024–25 season came to its conclusion. All had been linked with other clubs and none had committed themselves to the future of Liverpool F.C.

To lose three players of that calibre would be very damaging for any football club. To lose them and receive no income for them, worse.

But in April 2025 – as the team stormed towards its 20th league championship – news came from Anfield. Mo Salah had signed a contract extension. Then Van Dijk had done so too.

Great news for all Liverpool fans.

The future of the club was looking good. Very good.

ARNE SLOT

Manager

In the summer of 2024, when Arne Slot arrived at the AXA Training Centre in Kirkby, Merseyside, there was still a sense of sadness in the air.

Jürgen Klopp was gone. Klopp had been Liverpool manager for nine years and, as well as winning the Champions League and many other major honours, he had made Liverpool F.C. the English Champions, something that only four previous Liverpool managers – Bill Shankly, Bob Paisley, Joe Fagan, and Kenny Dalglish some 30 years earlier – had ever achieved before.

Arne Slot had to follow Klopp. But who is he?

Arne Slot is Dutch. He had been manager of Rotterdam club Feyenoord in the Dutch Eredivisie for three years, winning 98 games out of 150. In a league dominated by Ajax and PSV Eindhoven, Slot had guided Feyenoord to winning the Dutch league and cup, as well as reaching the final of the Europa Conference League.

So he had a pedigree. But would he be good enough to emulate Shankly, Paisley, Fagan, Dalglish and Klopp?

We know the answer to that now. But on 1 June 2024 we had no idea what the Dutchman was capable of.

KLOPP'S LAST TROPHY

League cup # 10

When the teams lined up for the 2024 EFL – or
Carabao – Cup final against Chelsea, Liverpool were
branded 'Klopp's Kids' by former Manchester United
legend, Gary Neville.

It was true Liverpool were being represented by a
young team. With Salah, Núñez, Alexander-Arnold
and Matip all injured, the line-up was inexperienced
– although they still had Virgil van Dijk as captain
and Kelleher in goal. And even though Kelleher was a
veteran of the 2022 final, he was still the number two
Liverpool keeper.

But both Virgil and Kelleher would prove to be
match winners.

With 118 minutes gone the game looked like it
would be just another 0–0 cup final, with another
penalty shootout.

As always, there had been plenty of goal-mouth action between the two rivals:

Chelsea's Raheem Sterling – hoping to haunt his former club – having a goal disallowed, correctly.

Liverpool's Gakpo hitting the post.

Then Virgil van Dijk having a goal disallowed, dubiously.

Next Conor Gallagher hit the post at the other end. And Chelsea were on top, as the game went into extra time. Kelleher had to make two excellent saves from Cole Palmer and Gallagher again, and was doubtless mentally preparing himself to face penalties.

Until the 118th minute. Until a late, perfect corner for Liverpool.

Tsimikas's delivery arrived close to the six-yard line. And there was Virgil van Dijk, leaping to head the ball across the Chelsea keeper into the goal mouth.

One-nil to Liverpool. Job done.